Business Process Management with a Business Rules Approach

Business Process Management with a Business Rules Approach

Implementing the Service Oriented Architecture

Tom Debevoise

Business Knowledge Architects, Incorporated

Business Knowledge Architects
Roanoke, Virginia 24019

Library of Congress Cataloging in Publication Data

These books are widely used by corporations and government agencies for training, marketing, and resale. The publisher offers discounts on this book when ordered in bulk quantities.

For more information, contact Corporate Sales Department.
Phone: 540-966-1036; FAX: 540-966-1045; E-mail: sales@bka-inc.com.com

Book design by Arbor Books
www.arborbooks.com

ISBN: 0-9769048-0-2
LCCN: 2005903977

Printed in Canada

To Barb

Contents

FOREWORD

Can you imagine a business, government agency or nonprofit organization that does not incorporate business processes into its operation? Every enterprise mission is defined by the processes' cyclical series of operations. Computer systems support many of these processes, and systems need accurate information in order to decide what to do. These decisions, then, mediate the flow of information between the actors in the enterprise. In the steps of the business process, managers and IT personnel refer to such mediators as *business rules*. Business rules specify how an entity will use information in its decision making process. Because business rules trigger critical decisions, and an organization's mission is achieved through the use of business processes, both need to be thoughtfully captured and preserved. If it were possible, wouldn't it be worthwhile to preserve business processes and business rules with software?

Every large organization or enterprise maintains in-house computer applications that perform business processes and apply business rules to data. These applications connect systems, users and their enterprise partners to ERP packages. The application is a critical part of the enterprise business process, yet it is difficult, and expensive, for the responsible teams to mold these applications around changes in processes and rules. This is because most applications are not created using a model of the business processes. Also, most IT shops are building applications using techniques or methods that predate Business Process Management (BPM) or Business Rules Approach (BR).

BPM and BR methods and software are not just technical jargon or high-tech hype. BPM and business rules are modern ways for teams to model the business process, business rules and the web services that serve the process. Today, there are plenty of available software packages that help to carry out BPM and business rules. Because most organizations manually manage their business processes, this software has business productivity benefits. It also improves an organization's productivity through business process reengineering.

With the IT budget of a commercial organization costing between 6-20 percent of its operating budget, one CIO magazine article estimates that 60% of this cost is for integration applications. I believe that BPM and BR dramatically cut the total cost of integration maintenance. It does this by cutting costs and providing productivity improvements.

I want to show you how you reduce the cost of integration with this new class of software: Business Process and Business Rules suites.

The long range benefit of this new approach occurs when the organization maintains its applications with an automated model of business processes and business rules. The savings arrive when an organization is smoothly able to adapt the business processes to its needs. BPM/BR eases that change because the vendors have designed this software with the flexibility to update and modernize your processes without the inefficient methods of the past.

Will the cost of this new method be a good investment? Nicholas Carr explains the case that information technology has become a commodity for business in his controversial *Harvard Business Review* article, "IT Doesn't Matter." In a study of 7,500 companies, those that spent the least on IT were among the top performers. This, and other analysis, led him to suggest that overspending is the greatest risk in IT. One way to cut the risk of overspending is for IT organizations to coordinate applications with a business model of the organization. To change a business rule or business process, you would simply change the model. This calls for a new architecture, a new class of integrated development environments and smarter, more agile organizations.

BPM/BR server tiers run in what the IT industry is calling the service oriented architecture (SOA). BPM/BR provides this so your IT management team easily changes parts of the technical infrastructure with the least disruption. This new approach uses separate servers for business processes and business rules. The SOA approach connects these by means of web services or messaging. In this text I am going to stress the web services approach. The advantage to the web services approach is that you might use them both internally and externally.

This book describes a strategy for combining Business Process Management and Business Rules Approach (BPM/BR). This is an approach that combines four interrelated trends in systems development: Business Rules, Business Process Management, Enterprise Integration (EI) and Business Intelligence (BI). Rather than give a laundry list of tasks and deliverables, I am going to recount a project that uses the BPM/BR. I hope that this will be an entertaining way of showing how to use this technique in your organization. I have developed a trial case for a construction equipment rental agency, Sumter Rents. I believe it will be small enough to cover in a book, yet show enough complexities to parallel the challenges organizations face.

Book Contents

I have divided this text into these chapters:

Introduction. The introduction presents the case of Sumter Rents. This mature business holds many challenges that I have drawn from my professional experience and the company that I work for, Business Knowledge Architects. I will describe how the service oriented economy and outsourcing movements raise the need for BPM. I will describe why we need a method that combines Business Process Management and Business Rules Approaches.

Chapter 2, Business Architecture. This chapter presents some of the challenges for the management at Sumter Rents. These challenges comprise conventional business rules and processes and present-day problems such as outsourcing services from other sellers. It also includes the use of a maintenance management module from an Enterprise Resource Planning (ERP) package. In this first phase, our team selects the objectives and goals of the project. They also develop a business case to justify the project. Typical of a business case, the participants in this task will develop what we want to reach for and what we will avoid. I will briefly describe a project management approach. The aim of the chapter is a firm foundation for a successful project.

Chapter 3, Business Process Management. This chapter describes how analysts build and improve the business processes for Sumter Rents. They prepare diagrams in Business Process Modeling Language (BPML). In a workshop setting, the project team improves and certifies the diagrams. The project plan's objectives include developing an equipment process and processing customer reservations. First, analysts develop core business processes. These high-level diagrams also detail how business rules apply the information. In this part of defining the business process, the analysts also develop the decision areas of the businesses rules analysis. The outcome of this step is business process diagrams.

Chapter 4, Business Rules. This chapter describes how the project team builds business rules for the Sumter Rents business processes. Earlier, the business process diagrams identified sets of business rules for the equipment maintenance and the customer folio. In workshops and interviews, our team develops the details of the business rules. As they finish the rules, a scribe models them into the business rules repository (BRR). Next, the systems administrators expose each business object as a web service. Lastly, the analyst connects the business process diagrams to the business object with a collaboration object that interacts with the web service. The outcome of this task is a system that is ready for testing and confirmation.

Chapter 5, Business Intelligence. This chapter describes how the business processes and business rules activities of the Sumter Rents project create and maintain the data warehouse. The first purpose of the BI system is to estimate an ideal rental inventory, one that matches projected customer demand. The project also supports business activity monitoring. The business rules in the BRR affect the design of the data warehouse. Business processes provide new information about customer behavior and retail performance. Your BPM software includes internal process timing information that you distill into efficiency metrics. The outcome of this activity is a data warehouse that helps managers understand what is happening in Sumter Rents.

Chapter 6, IT Convergence. Business Process management offers a powerful way to manage your legacy systems. If you have many legacy systems and many systems administrators, then there is a good chance that much of what they do can be managed by BPM software. This is called IT convergence. This chapter describes how to convert your legacy processes to a BPM environment. I describe how to add controls, error reporting and logging standards. This development effort is not extensive. The controls I suggest adding are the ones that your organization does manually. As you add support for legacy processes to Business Process Management, you start to add more advanced business processes to your environment.

Business Process Management puts a great deal of control in the hands of managers. Chapter 7 also describes process management.

Chapter 7, Technical Architecture. In this chapter, I present characteristics of a technical architecture for the service oriented environment. In previous chapters, I described two side effects of the new service oriented economy: Competitive companies outsource inefficient activities to cut cost. And they publish their products and services on the internet. A team uses the BPM/BR method to design flexible business processes that do this. However, the organization's architecture must also be flexible. This chapter describes the mission of the different tiers of the technical oriented architecture.

Chapter 8, Transition. This chapter briefly covers some of the considerations of putting the project into production. A quality assurance team should test all business processes against valid data to confirm or deny that the system properly performs the business rules and processes. To avoid production issues, the team should also load test the entire application. I will describe how a configuration management group works with a Business Process Management approach and a business rules repository. The goal of this chapter is the goal of the project, a new production system.

Chapter 9, Conclusion. To close the book, I predict the benefits achieved by an enterprise that creates an information technology environment from a model of how the business works. I believe that this will change the economics of the organization. Business modeling is an improvement over other forms of software engineering. However since modeling a business is fundamentally different from modeling data or objects, IT teams are certain to face a certain culture shock.

Suggested Reading Patterns. This textbook has two central tracks. The first is a tale description of a project that uses the BPM/BR to complete a project. The next is an exposition which presents technical details of what organization needs to understand.

You do not need to read every chapter to gain some benefit from this book. If you are a manager considering the use of a BPM and business rules and want to get a feel for how it would benefit your organization, then read chapters 1 through 5. After the introductions the chapters answer these questions:

- Chapter 2 Business Architecture: What are the business systems problems that need addressing? What is the justification for the projects? When are we going to do them?
- Chapter 3 Business Process Management: What are the basic business processes that will construct the project solutions? How are we going to incorporate business rule architecture?
- Chapter 4 Business Rules: How do we discern and extract the business rules for our application? How do we implement in the Business Rules Software?
- Chapter 5 Business Intelligence: How do we improve executive decisions? What are the metrics for the decisions? What is the relationship between the business rule, business processes and the Data Warehouse?

- Chapter 6 IT Convergence: How to we manage legacy systems in a business processing environment? How do we move legacy systems into the environment? What are the benefits to centralized management?
- Chapter 7 Transition: How do we create and deploy the application? How do we create a safe and stable system?

For the division manager, chapters 2, 3 and 6 describe how a significant portion of the IT infrastructure may be reengineered.

The BPM/BR is a new way of completing integration projects. I feel it is the only application development approach that addresses the key objectives of enabling organizations to create comprehensive, industry-specific business processes while reducing the cost, complexity, and time of cross-application integration.

The BPM/BR approaches move application integration from a complex and expensive technical challenge into a simple way to build applications for the enterprise and its customers and partners. The approach provides an integrated process control architecture that achieves real-time visibility into parts of the business process. Not only do the integrated business rules and process control tactics enable organizations to place business processes quickly, they also yield the flexibility to adapt processes in response to fast-changing operational dynamics.

The objective of this approach is to create a single point of "plug and play" at a high-level. Organizations are not locked into the rigid architecture of an integration that they have painfully created. They have the freedom to choose services from other companies and change applications and technology. Through a business rules and integrated process control strategy, organizations finally realize the strategic benefits of full and flexible application integration at dramatically reduced cost, complexity, and time to deployment. This is the true nature of the agile organization.

I hope that we have presented a good portion of the way forward with this text. There are tools and machinery in this book that will help designers seeking to improve their work. The objective of the BPM/BR methods is to provide teams with the ability to build and control new systems that live with changing, abstract business models.

For news about the book and author please go to www.BKA-INC.com

Thanks

I want to thank all of the people that helped me with this project over the past few months including Buddy Towne, Warren Capps, Tim Clotworthy, George Sarris, and Cindy Shearer.

I want to especially thank Jim Bromhal for his many suggestions.

References

Carr, Nicolas G, 2003 "IT Doesn't Matter", Boston MA, Harvard Business Review.

INTRODUCTION

Is your IT infrastructure ready to respond to economic slowdowns, globalization, and outsourcing movements? What role would you play if your company or government agency moved a division offshore or privatized something? To help with the critical role of process management, leading software companies have released new types of software, especially solutions for Business Process Management (BPM) and Business Rules Approach (BR). A business process is a repeating cycle that reaches a business goal. Business rules mediate the information in the business process. BPM and BR software support business goals by managing and running business processes and business rules. This class of software simplifies changes. They help your organization become more competitive by allowing you to respond to opportunities by simply adapting your business to the new world. But your IT organization must change its methods to use BPM or BR software. The biggest change is conceptual—your software designers will no longer describe what the software does; they will describe what the business does.

BPM is responsible for lowering the boundary between the brick walls of businesses and the networked global economy. Through BPM, the most competitive companies are forging a close relationship with their customers and suppliers. The enterprise application integration (EAI) industry calls closely related groups of business services a "composite application." The composite application combines the services of everyone's systems into a virtual application. To build a composite application, you need to be able to expose your system services. There are two important standards for performing this—the web services description language (WSDL) and the Business Process Execution Language (BPEL). When you develop your composite application with these languages, you create a Service Oriented Architecture (SOA). Your IT organization needs a combination of Business Process Management and Business Rules Approach (BPM/BR) to build the composite application in an SOA.

Sumter Rents is a leading construction equipment rental firm in the Southeast U.S. This company provides short and long-term rental of heavy or specialized construction equipment to small, midsized and fortune

500 companies. Sumter also leases smaller machinery and specialized hand tools to the consumer.

The construction rental market is a growing and profitable part of Sumter's business. Since the slowdown in the economy, construction firms have augmented their fleets with leases of varying terms. This strategy has allowed many construction firms to cut their capitalized costs. Also, smaller companies use leasing of construction equipment as leverage to aim for larger projects and other opportunities that they might not otherwise chase. Because contractor rentals are the largest part of their revenue, Sumter Rents wants to expand their share of this market. In Europe, construction firms lease up to 80% of their heavy equipment. Sumter sees a parallel opportunity for growth potential in the American rental market.

Sumter Rents, Inc. has over 30 years of experience in the field. They lease and service over 700 types of equipment including a wide range of bulldozers, backhoes, compaction rollers, work platforms (cherry pickers), cranes, air compressors, generators and paving equipment. Other types of equipment include mobile storage and pumping equipment. Also, they lease smaller equipment to the homeowner market including Bobcats, tractors and hand tools.

Sumter's IT department has recently converted their legacy accounting systems into SAP R3. Sumter also uses the SAP Plant Maintenance (SAP PM) application. SAP PM is a software solution that potentially covers all maintenance tasks for Sumter. SAP PM plans and tracks all maintenance for system availability, costs, materials, and personnel placement.

Sumter wants to create a closer relation with their customers by providing them with rental and related information services on the Internet. Sumter understands that a service-oriented architecture is a key competitive technology in the current economy. As we will see, there are several key areas where Sumter will benefit from this business approach.

Sumter Rents: New Service Oriented Offerings

In foraging a deeper alliance with the construction companies, Sumter imagines a web services model that will connect the rental fleet with the customer's project and bid planning. Sumter intends to offer special discounts to these "special partners." One of the keys is for Sumter to identify high volume customers and to offer discounted pricings via web services to these customers. In exchange for registering, special partners will get a spreadsheet with a .NET pricing page that they use for planning projects. The hope is that customers will rapidly negotiate corporate contract terms that will grow the contractor's business as well as Sumter's rental business.

Sumter has integrated SAP with an old fashioned hub-and-spoke IT environment. Their previous development methods buried processes and rules in many COBOL (80's), PL*SQL (90's) and ASP (00's) applications. Also, the old ways have scattered integration programs across their technical architecture. The current IT team knows it will need to adapt quickly to the process changes that they need a web services model. The business will need custom business processes for the preferred partners. Sumter wants to be able to change processes and rules so it can publish its new offerings on the internet. With processes and rules buried in the compute code, it is difficult for them to do this.

Business Process Management and Business Rules Meet Today's Challenges

Sumter Rents plans to overcome the difficulties of changing processes and rules by using a combination of Business Process Management and Business Rules Approach (BPM/BR). Sumter hopes to develop a useful environment for customers and managers that will be easy to modify as business needs change. Organizations do this with a combination of commercial software and BPM/BR.

BPM/BR organizes integration into two separate areas: an environment of software and server(s) that is responsible for business processes, and another environment that is responsible for business rules. This arrangement simplifies updates to new software releases. The chief benefit of this is that there is a "zero administration" capability because processes and rules are positioned for change. Another benefit is that the BPM/BR changes an organization's methods because it needs radically fewer personnel and shorter project cycles.

"Zero administration" for items that are positioned for change does not mean that they should not be thoroughly tested. It does mean that the change is easier to make.

Business Process Management (BPM) Defined

A business process is a sequence of activities that carries out a complete business goal. For example, when a customer fills out an order form, you would not consider it complete until the interface program posted the order to the ERP. Business Process Management is the identification, understanding and management of business processes that link with people and systems in and across organizations.

There are plenty of new software packages that use Business Process Management to create *systems*. Examples include Tibco™, SeeBeyond™ and WebMethods™.

Business Rule Approach Defined

A business rule is a mediator of information in computer systems for decision makers, such as managers, employees and salespeople. Business rules decide with information. When you change the business rule, you change the decisions. A business rule can be a policy, a constraint or a regulatory requirement. An example of a business rule would be to filter the information needed to decide whether to extend credit to a customer. There are new classes of software that can take a group of business rules and create an entire application. Examples include Concordia™ and Pega™.

The Business Rules Approach is a new design technique for formalizing an enterprise's critical business rules in a language the manager and technologist understand. Business rules create an unambiguous statement of what a business does with information to decide a proposition. The formal specification becomes information for process and rules engines to run. The language should be legible by the application engines. The clauses of the language include terms, data, translations, procedures and processes. The outcome of this procedure is metadata that describes the steps of a given rule, and is evaluated by engines. The result is a tool that collects, analyzes and models business rules and produces applications that implement them. The technical approach described here offers a strategic first step in modernizing the method of creating connected, not interfaced, technology solutions.

Composing the Service Oriented Architecture with BPM/BR

A Service Oriented Architecture (SOA) is both a design approach to information technology and a basic business strategy. A *service* in SOA is a piece of a computer system packaged as a reusable ingredient for use in a business process. The .NET spreadsheet that Sumter plans to use is a good example of this. Business process management (BPM) is a good strategy for modeling the processes and identifying opportunities for competitive improvement in an enterprise. The SOA connects the BPM to the customer or trading partner.

BPM visualizes the current business as an "information chain." An information chain connects a step-by-step series of activities with data. Think of the information chain as a macro business process and SOA as the links. The process of construction contractors bidding on projects and performing services is an example. Sumter aims to be a tighter part of the information chain by forging a closer relation with the contractors. As the value of a particular service of the business becomes clearer, managers outsource or cutout services. The business offers its special services and products to customers.

Service Oriented Businesses Need a Composite Method

If you are working with business systems such as the one we described for Sumter, then consider the new methods offered by Business Process Management and Business Rules Approach. Today, I believe that these techniques should be an important part of your delivery methods. This chapter will show you how Business Process Management and Business Rules Approach (BPM/BR) has worked and how it will work for you.

My Experience with Changing Methodology

As an engineer with more than twenty years of experience, I develop ways of connecting business needs with technological capacities. I've developed:

- Computer applications for environmental modeling, automated data collection and supervisory control and data acquisition (SCADA) systems
- Diagnostics programs using expert systems, an artificial intelligence technique that analyzed a user's questions and provided probable solutions
- Maintenance Management databases for public infrastructures, water, sewer and storm water systems that selected what to do with the different conditions of pipes, pumps, valves and other parts.
- An enterprise clinical trial system, a cross-trial system that generated case report forms and stored data for the FDA's multiphase process
- Inventory management, specifically downstream integration for the petroleum industry

I've had different roles in these projects, including developer, designer, systems administrator and manager. In these roles, I've met many different types of organizational needs, and different design approaches to data and information processing. I've always been a part of organizations that solved problems by designing and programming computer applications.

My early career in 'hard engineering' taught me the value of rigorous design methods

Because application development is complex and challenging work, I have always sought to use the best design techniques for finishing my projects. My background in "hard" engineering taught me that doing a project with a disciplined design method must be a core value in my work.

Experience has taught me that creative project teams adapt current tools and method to the needs of the project. For instance, some organizations have a greater need for explaining and agreeing to written requirements than others. Other projects need fewer group workshops because hardware interface controls drive the needs of that project, and there is little human involvement.

BPM/BR Describes the Business, Not the Technical Details

Business processes and business rules describe the business, not the technical details. I will show how these new design methods meet Sumter's challenges. Also, I will show how they work together to make it simple for an organization to update rules or processes without complicated redeployments of production systems.

BPM/BR represents a change in the language and symbols that we use to describe information systems—these methods have become more business-centered and less tied to the technical details of systems. In the past, the IT industry has moved first from information engineering (IE), to object oriented software engineering (OOSE), to "Use Case" analysis. Along the way, commercial off-the-shelf (COTS) software became an important part of commonly used technology. The latest methods changed the focus from mathematical theories of data and functions into pictures and English sentences of what the business does. For instance: IE uses an entity relationship diagram (ERD). The ERD depicts *relational calculus* formulas. A business process diagram looks and acts like a white board, and business rules have written descriptions.

In the late 1980's and early 1990's my practice focused on relational databases, and I did much of the design work with data modeling. James Martin's information engineering (IE), a data-centered approach, soon became a prevalent practice, and it spread throughout the IT industry. Some believed there were innate weaknesses in a "data-centric" approach. Data models are rigid depictions of the last step of a part of a process. A data model needs programs to create records in the data. As the database changes, the programs that feed the database need to change as well. Next, object-oriented software engineering (OOSE) arose to compete with IE. Both of these old methods have many adherents to this day, yet neither of them connects business rules and business processes to the organizations applications.

By the late 1990's I was working with focused, solution-oriented software including Business Intelligence (BI), supply chain management (SCM), and customer relationship management (CRM). Increasingly, every project that I work with involves integrating large systems COTS software. These customers develop and maintain fewer of their own applications by setting up COTS packages. They are making these changes because:

- Developing equivalent systems in-house is too expensive.
- Commercial software improves the quality of the environment.
- Commercial software carries out competitive commercial practices.

Each need for integration involves business rules and business processes. With IE or OOSE, the developers buried rules and processes into their computer programs.

Data modeling and use case analysis create a technical snapshot of how the organization does business today. Businesses always need to change their processes and rules to remain competitive. Data Modeling, and even use case analysis, does not easily help with these changes in applications. So in some ways, BPM/BR software is the next step in modern software. Instead of writing programs in Java or C, BPM/BR organizations model what the business does in words and diagrams. To update the process or rule, you update the diagrams and words.

In many industries–telecommunications, finance, and healthcare–almost every process already has set up a data model. What these industries want to do is improve through cutting the cost of implementing new practices. They have begun to see the need for modeling the processes and the rules that feed their COTS packages. They are using service oriented architecture (SOA) to offer these processes to customers as a service.

People and Organizations Need to Change to Move to BPM/BR

The SOA presents a big challenge to the mature IT organization. The practice of software design has shifted its focus many times during the last twenty years, and the teams doing the work have a hard time following. The exploding powers of software and hardware capacity also contributed to this. Organizations have struggled to use modern technology, and it will be a struggle for them to move to an SOA.

In my career, I have often witnessed poor management choices with technology. For instance, in the mid 1990's, at one Telco, I met a team of at least eighteen developers working to build their own database; even though most organization had long since moved to commercial databases. Perhaps you have also worked in organizations that have expended efforts for developing software that is already commercially available.

The database development team situation seems outrageous. But, even today, I meet teams that develop portals, process managers and workflow solutions.

I have found that new application development methods need to be coupled with changes in the IT groups. Supporters of the new methods face a tough challenge: how to insert new ways of building applications into organizations who say that the older ways of doing business are still valuable or successful.

I've decided that computing technology develops much faster than humans! What I've noted is that while it is possible for a software package to offer a better, faster, and cheaper way of developing an application, it is very difficult for a group of people in an organization to change their ways to take advantage of it.

Even when organizations know of better ways to meet their IT challenges, it is difficult for them to change course and adopt them. I have heard managers compare their team's performance to a battleship's turning radius. They say that it might take a long time to turn around and change their direction when information technology and business are moving in one direction. Even so, you have to be wondering how groups that are in charge of mission critical systems will use BPM, SOA, and business rules.

In the eighties and nineties, software engineering provided methods and tools to simplify development, configuration and testing. These development environments aided creating screens, databases and reports. However, you probably know that poorly used client-server tools, such as Sybase's PowerBuilder or Borland's Delphi, could put too many business rules in the client-side programs. In these tools, programmers put business rules code in the programs that ran the screens and reports. Hundreds or thousands of personal computers run these programs. On each computer would be a version of the application and "run-time" software. A change to the business rules in the application code calls for expensive and painful redeployments of the client-server application. To change a business rule, the IT group has to redeploy the updated program to all client computers.

Web technology did not solve the problem of changes to client-server business rules. If programmers did not properly develop a web application, then they did not position the business rules for simple changes. SOA moves the entire industry a step closer to an agile business.

Organizations Need an Agile Architecture: the Service Oriented Architecture

Because their current IT systems do not meet their objectives, the expectations of executive management can be both ahead of the organization's abilities and behind the best competitive strategy. Management is taking these steps to improve the alignment:

- Adopting business process approaches to improve operations.
- Offering portions of the business process to customers and trading partners.
- Adopting commercial software packages.
- Replacing or changing the legacy systems and processes; exposing the abilities of the systems to in-house systems and customers.

Many organizations are striving to coordinate their business needs and their IT environment. Many enterprises are using Business Intelligence and data warehousing to improve analytical decision making and reporting requirements. They use commercial software for customer relationship management (CRM), supply chain management (SCM), enterprise resource planning (ERP) and other areas. The risk is that organizations may have poorly added BI, CRM, SCM or ERP into their system.

As businesses replace outdated or noncompetitive systems, they move processes and rules from the old systems into the integration programs. Executive management wants to improve the processes and rules. The problem is that the further back you go in time, the more difficult it is to change the process or rules. This is because either the old design documentation is cryptic and incomplete, or someone must read and understand mysterious computer programs written in COBOL or C.

Because executive management expects systems to be able to adapt tactical changes in processes and rules, the way your organization adds COTS software to the system is an important choice. For this technical choice to be effective, you need to decide how to make technical systems work seamlessly with your business objectives. You need a virtual blueprint that effectively combines strategies and methods that handle changes in business rules and processes. The scheme should also preserve your investment in the best software and systems.

An adaptable solution, one that would be more agile, would be a combination of BPM software such as SeeBeyond™, Tibco™, or WebMethods™ and business rules software such as Pega™ or Corticon™. This combination builds an agile architecture—one that easily allows changes.

Web Services' Role in the Agile Architecture

The emerging power of web services is a key to agile architectures. Web services are agile because you change them without changing the client programs. The web services model is an effective architecture for the system that handles an enterprise. Web services are flexible because they integrate with a program as a client application, or they act as server for many clients. This means that a web service acts like a mini web-server for your integration programs. For example, there are web services that confirm European addresses. You could use the service in a program that validates an address before printing a shipping label. Client applications use these with a minimum amount of programming.

A web service is a software system designed to support interoperable machine-to-machine interaction over a network. Web services employ industry standards so that they are compatible with many types of programming languages. XML documents describe web services in a format known as web services description language (WSDL). This is a new idea because a WSDL describes how a system takes advantage of the solutions that are on the internet or intranet.

Web services promise to create systems that are open and adaptable. IT teams solve problems such as creating new business rules, processes or interfaces. Once you solve these problems, you publish the solution to other applications as a WSDL. The web service is visible inside the enterprise or outside, to the internet. You might reuse the solution in other applications without rewriting the code. Because WSDL is a standard, it is easy to understand how to use the service.

Business Process Execution Language and the Composite Application

Business Process Extended Language (BPEL) extends Web services in an important way. BPEL orchestrates a collection of WSDLs. For example, the WSDLs involved in setting up contracts with a trading partner may involve activities such as "validate contract info" and "bid on contract" integrated with vendor downstream legacy systems. In the web services architecture, each of the WSDLs has specific inputs and outputs and BPEL composes them. This is important because without an underlying orchestration, individual web services are just individual instruments.

BPEL exposes services and powers that developers previously buried in systems. Without BPEL, the IT team must develop complicated interfaces that use hidden services and capacities. BPEL strengthens web services and allows them to work with one another. BPEL orchestration also manages business processes. BPEL specifies steps that the business process automatically performs. The benefit of this is that BPEL:

- Removes complex interfaces.
- Improves, changes or cuts out unnecessary steps.
- Reuses functionality with powers that BPEL publishes in the WSDL.
- Makes costly code reengineering unnecessary.
- Outsources business processes
- Offers portions of the process a service to other customers.

Composite applications are orchestrations of different programs and systems that act as one application. You use BPEL to create the *Composite Application*. In this book, I am going to describe the role of business processes and business rules in the composite application.

Transition to the Way Forward

So, there are many benefits to building a composite application in an SOA. If you do it right, you can be competitive, and customers and trading partners will want to do business with you. I have found that this new environment is more agile and less costly to build and maintain. What we need is a method for getting there. My suggestion is that we use a composite method, one that combines BPM and business rules.

Process for a Composite Method

Creating and running the IT environment is a process. In the spirit of BPM, we consider a process that uses BPM and business rules to do this differently from IE or OOSE. The difference is that you view systems, such as ERP, as a provider of services. With BPM/BR, you define how your business uses the services.

The BPM/BR is a method that combines business rules, business process management and architectural approaches. Collectively, these bring business rules, business processes and other IT parts together in one step. In the same spirit, the BPM/BR encourages the businesses to use COTS software.

Figure 1.1 presents a business process diagram of the BPM/BR. This figure introduces the business process model idea. A business process is an orchestration of activities that finishes an important aim or purpose. This process diagram outlines the BPM/BR method. The diagram depicts the activities by labeled boxes. If the box has small squares in it, then the diagram hides details beneath the process. Because they are high level, I have collapsed the activities. I will expand most activities in the coming chapters. The arrows show the flow from activity to activity. The circle depicts the state of the activity with a starting activity and an ending state. At the top of the vertical "swim-lanes," the diagram labels the groups responsible for the various activities. The diagram shows decisions as diamonds or pointy boxes. Parallel activities go on concurrently. They branch from the horizontal lines which flow to the activities they spawn.

With the process activities shown on figure 1.1, the BPM/BR team creates the models for a solution that either carries out or updates a business process. The business processes and business rules create user interfaces, business-to-business integration, COTS integration and data warehouse ingredients. The metadata that describes these become important artifacts of the BPM/BR approach.

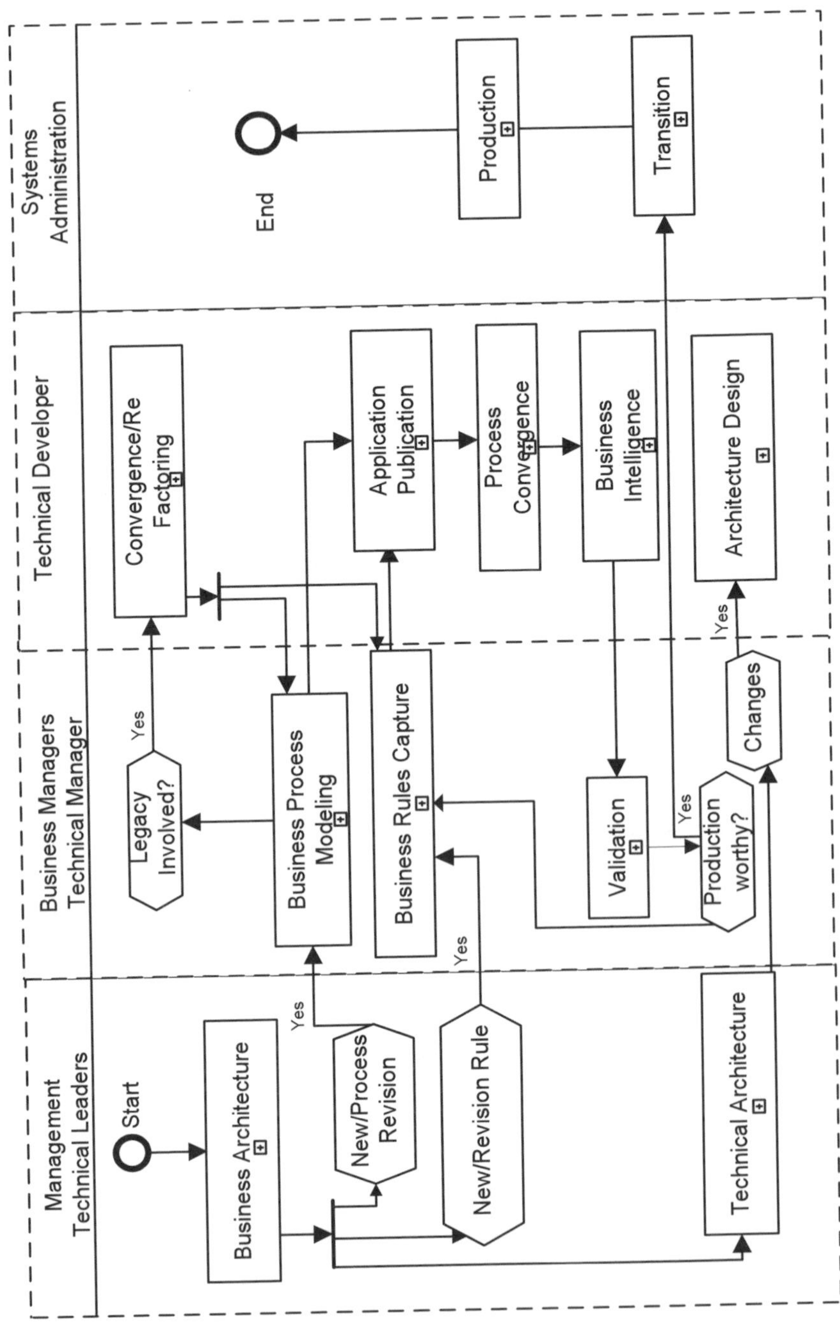

Figure 1.1 This business process diagram depicts the twelve basic activities in the BPM/BR.

The BPM/BR approach creates data-driven specifications (metadata) of an application's work. The Business Rules Approach stores business rules as data in a database (metadata). BPM stores business processes as Business Process Modeling Language (BPML) in the BMP repository.

BPML also:

- Chooses and sequences activities.
- Handles system errors or exceptions.
- Handles process errors through compensations.

For instance, a business process for a loan approval system might need to outsource employment verification to an external firm. An organization that uses BPM changes the process for handling this by changing the business process diagram.

The BPM/BR approach also preserves investments in the older systems that they wish to keep by exposing their services on the web. BPML is independent of the language or system that provides service to a process. So it easily uses the legacy application as an activity.

There are many benefits to storing business rules as metadata in a business rules repository (BRR). Because a BRR works through sentences and data, you easily change the language to produce a needed product. Because the sentences in the BRR are simple to read, non-technical managers are able to update them. For instance, a contracting organization might have policies allowing a customer to order an item from several different trading partner contracts. In another contracting scenario, there could be rules for payment of different transport types —based on the final destination. Business rules and processes are simple to create and update when the business expresses their processes in BPML, and their policies in English words. BPML software creates BPEL to run the process, and the phrases of business rules run the steps that enforce them. In the example, the business user changes the sentence that specifies some orders assigned to a contract, or they add a new transport mechanism. The result is that it is faster to update the responsible applications.

Throughout a BPM/BR process cycle, project managers need to oversee how well the team carries out the objectives, the extent of progress and how efficiently the organization finishes cycles. Project managers need to direct and measure the efforts of a team with specific roles and responsibilities.

Here, I want to describe the highlights of the activities shown in figure 1.1. Because business process repositories and business rules repositories are recent technologies, the outcome of the activities feeds into the others in a new way. There is a new type of output in each of the activities: business processes, business rules, Business Intelligence and technical architecture.

BPM/BR Process Activities

Of the basic activities in diagram 1, the five critical activities are:

- *Business Architecture*: The management team addresses the strategic and tactical goals of the business in a way that leverages the new world of business processes. The activity has steps for identifying services that the business should publish or use in their composite application. The outcome of the business architecture is a portfolio of projects.
- *Business Process Modeling*: For each project that improves the business architecture, the technical/management team creates a prototype of a business process model. To do this, the team first builds a high-level visual model in Business Process Modeling Language (BPML). BPML looks a bit like the diagrams that people draw on white boards: a collection of boxes and arrows. Each box represents an activity and the lines and arrows represent the streams of information between them.
- *Business Rules Capture:* The Business Rules Approach specifies the business process validation needs in a precise language. Through discovery processes such as workshop sessions, the language incrementally builds business rules. The aim is to foster a method that simplifies the maintenance of the application.
- *Business Intelligence*: Business Intelligence is a natural outcome of the BPM/BR method. You compose a data warehouse from the business rules, processes, and transactions in the business process. Much of the information needed for a data schema for the data warehouse arises from information you gathered in the previous steps. Often you need to support a statistical decision model, and this will guide you. However, there are intrinsic data warehouse powers to every transactional system.
- *Technical Architecture*: The aim of BPM is to break the barriers between IT and business. If this is your aim, you will need to modernize your technical architecture and simplify its administration. The types of software I am describing improve the connection between business tactics and applications.

In summary, the BPM/BR orchestrates business and IT. By orchestrate, I mean the systems do what the business needs them to do, not what legacy systems developers had it do. This method provides business managers with the information technology they need. The BPM/BR approach combines Business Rules Approach and Business Process Management into a unified approach. I will describe how these new tools improve construction of the operational system, data warehousing and the integration process. The result is a powerful system that saves the organization's time and money by allowing it to run the system with a smaller, more skilled staff and shorter development cycles.

The BPM/BR modernizes the way you build today's business information architectures. It replaces outmoded ways of developing the IT environment. Before, IT would cobble together competitive, once-leading-edge technologies on the IT ecosystem with hardwired methods. These retrofits resulted in a rigid technical architecture. The BPM/BR overcomes this by addressing integration, Business Intelligence and systems in one process. It avoids retrofitting the environment by creating loosely coupled business processes that simply add new solutions, commercial software or analytical tools.

Success with BPM/BR

In 2000, the Department of Defense faced a challenge. It rapidly needed to deploy an inventory management system to almost ninety wholesale fuel distribution centers around the world. These centers had low numbers of transactions each month (fewer than 50). The Defense Logistics Agency (DLA) management faced the potential cost of deploying an aging, thick client application at a cost of over $2.7M. The company I am associated with, Business Knowledge Architects, was responsible for the integration server. We'd taken a Business Rules Approach to developing interfaces and the data warehouse. We were able to use the techniques described in this textbook to create a web application.

In fewer than 60 days, the application was quickly tested and put into production. The implementation has been a success and has been deployed to over 150 locations worldwide. We saved the DOD over $4M.

Summary

- Competitive businesses are forging closer alliances with their customers and trading partners. An important way to do this is to expose their offerings on the internet.
- To remain competitive, businesses must rapidly adapt their business processes and business rules.

- A business rule is a mediator of a business decision.
- A business process is a sequence of activities that achieves a goal.
- Enterprise architecture has changed over the last decade. There is more use of COTS and data warehouses. One of the most expensive line items in an Enterprise IT budget is integration. It is expensive to combine these elements.
- Old design methods are steeped in mathematical terminology that only a few understood. The methods of Business Process Management and Business Rules improve the way technical teams design business systems. These new methods describe what the business does, not what the computer systems do.
- Business Process Management and the Service Oriented Architecture (SOA) is not only a technical innovation, it is a business strategy. BPM and SOA will be a critical part of the outsourcing revolution.
- Web services are a critical part of the SSO.
- The BPM/BR method is a process for developing systems that integrate their systems internally and externally. The process also exposes a business's services on the internet.

References

Smith, Howard and Fingar, Peter, 2003, *Business Process Management*, Tampa Florida, Meghan-Kiffer Press.

Ross, Ronald G, 2003, Principles of the Business Rule Approach, Addison-Wesley.

The WS-BPEL specification is located at *http://cvs.sourceforge.net/viewcvs.py/wsbpeltc/*

CHAPTER TWO

Business Architecture

How do you begin to realize the vision of the SOA, with all the IT refuse of past 20+ years around you? I suggest you spend some time thinking about what your enterprise should look like in a BPM world. I call this step the business architecture, and during this phase, projects are planned for connecting your business into the networked, service-oriented economy.

Previously, businesses produced products from the ground up—companies created parts, assembled them, sent them to market, and then sold them directly to customers. This model is rapidly disappearing. Most large industries have outsourced everything from parts manufacturing to customer financing. In the Harvard Business Review article entitled "Will You Survive the Outsourcing Revolution?" Uday Karmarkar argues that competitive businesses exist because of their position in an information chain. The information chain is a network of services for transactions and queries searching for the most efficient use of capitol in the economy. To take part, a company, individual or government must expose and incorporate their services into many composite applications. In other words, your customers should incorporate your special offerings into their processes. To me, this sounds like the old academic axiom: "publish or perish." Your potential customers will go elsewhere if they don't know that you have services that they need. BPM is the emerging method for publishing and outsourcing a business's services and connecting these with others.

The business case that we are studying is a good example of how outsourcing affects business tactics. First, businesses leased equipment because they needed short-term resources. Lately, to cut their capitalized cost, construction companies lease a portion or part of their fleet. Construction businesses can be more competitive when they augment their fleet with leases. In another example, Sumter Rents is selling their fleet maintenance capacities to third party organizations.

Clearly, the composite application plays a role in the information chain. The composite architecture must be agile in order adapt to business changes and take advantage of economic opportunities. The business architecture manages a Service Oriented Architecture that connects the business to the service oriented economy.

Sumter has 70 leasing outlets throughout the South with some operations in the Midwest. With the rise in the rental industry they have experienced rapid growth, and in the last fiscal year they turned over $220M in revenue.

Through years of maintaining a large fleet of equipment, Sumter has developed a skilled maintenance department. Their reputation in this area is so great that some manufacturers have outsourced their service care to them. Sumter's customers have also begun to outsource the care and maintenance of their fleets of equipment.

Sumter's growth has come at a cost. Sumter has bought 20 smaller rental firms, and integrating these companies has not been easy. The new maintenance staff is skilled, yet their practices are inconsistent. Sumter prides itself on being able to do business with a wide range of customers, yet the regional offices often have a problem balancing inventory and sharing equipment. When stores do not share equipment, the company disappoints customers and loses revenue. In addition, the customer service team has not efficiently scheduled and delivered equipment to customers.

As I wrote in the introduction, Sumter Rents uses SAP's Plant Maintenance module (SAP PM) as an automated fleet maintenance solution. SAP PM has had benefits, yet there have been miscues in work orders. Because usage hours (how many hours on the odometer) drives the maintenance schedules of most heavy equipment, data entry errors might cause SAP PM to produce mistaken work orders. Not every Sumter retail branch is properly using the powers of SAP PM. The current process needs much manual effort. They need a simpler process.

Sumter has a good web presence for their customers. Customers can view their account information including accounts receivable and the equipment that they have out on rent. However, they can't order equipment or see when the equipment that they need will become available. Customers have asked that the web be able to alert them when named types of equipment are available. Increasingly, customers want to seek certified operators with their equipment. Using its relationship with several labor contractors, Sumter hopes to increase its services by allowing customers to order labor.

Sumter's Business Objectives and Strategy

The CEO of Sumter is David Edmond Burk III. David is the grandson of the founder and majority shareholder.

As the CEO, David's goal is to build his business from fourth place to third place in the southeast. He aims to do this by improving the customer's rental experience. He has developed a three-step plan of action:

- Become the commercial customer's best partner in the rental industry through an extended partnership, from project planning to operator staffing and efficient delivery.
- Become the premier source for equipment fleet maintenance. Offer a comprehensive plan for fleet maintenance using the SAP PM system.
- Keep an inventory of the most modern fleet of equipment available, by accurately assessing the need for new rentals and by timely selling their existing fleet at the best price.

David is a visionary in his field, and he grasps the complexities of what he wants his team to do. In some of his meetings he describes an ideal environment with all problems solved. Some of his visions have included:

- Provide model service for all lease orders. Incorporate the customer's reasoning in the order details, bid orders, and equipment mobilization. Create a single, predictable fee for mobilizing equipment.
- Use radio frequency identification (RFID) to verify the equipment's run hours; download the information from the engine information module.
- Plan efficient transportation and mobilization of all equipment flatbeds so that they roll from store to customers with the fullest possible loads.
- Create a model of when to sell equipment, and take advantage of offshore variation in prices while balancing rental income from depreciated equipment.

David wants to improve the balance of in-store inventory and the business process of reselling used equipment. Rapidly rising prices in China, and other areas, create the opportunity to rotate out older equipment. This economic analysis would better match the company's inventory with sales demands and improve the age of the overall Sumter fleet. Sumter Rents might dispose of equipment at a profit; however, they must balance the numbers against the rental income, cost of sales, and the service to the customer. The current system is not rigorous enough to adequately handle such calculations, and is largely based on out-of-date information and many managers' guesses. Dave thinks these areas should be more carefully analyzed.

Sumter's Business Challenges

Successful leaders focus on opportunities. Therefore, business challenges should first address opportunities, then problems next. I frame a business challenge as a circumstance or question, which—supplied with effort, information, people or capital—results in a capitalized opportunity. Secondarily, a business challenge is a circumstance or question that might result in a solved problem.

These are Sumter Rents top business challenges:

1. Sales and Customer Service is improved with more information from the customer portal that already exists.
2. Sumter Rents needs to develop a closer partnership with its largest customers.
3. Sumter Rents aims to develop a revenue source by servicing the customer-owned equipment.

When a customer's needed equipment is unavailable, he will often look elsewhere. To offset this tendency, Sumter could notify customers when their needed equipment becomes available. Some customers even want this announcement sent to their mobile computers. Sumter Rents aims to give this information in a timely and interactive way.

Additionally, when customers use the portal, Sumter could suggest productivity improvements targeted and useful to the customers. The payoff for Sumter Rents is that it improves its rental income by providing companion rental equipment and services for the customer's job. The suggestions may include:

- Scheduling equipment operators from labor trading partners.
- Building small business cases for more expensive, yet more efficient rental selections.

Sumter Rents' biggest challenge is gaining a closer partnership with its best customers—the large construction firms. These companies lease equipment for longer periods and significantly lengthen the lease periods. This improves the profitability of rental units. Sumter intends to use its services and information systems to tighten its partnership with these businesses. So, the customer should be able to plan for a project—even months in advance, when he is preparing a project bid. Traditionally, in a web model, a contractor might download a price list and copy the data into a spreadsheet. Next, the contractor prepares his bid including material, labor mobilization, site preparation and equipment.

What the new service oriented model suggests is that this price list should be loaded into the spreadsheet as a .NET component. In fact, Sumter has been pondering a new "rental process" spreadsheet that would combine the price list, notices of needed equipment, and suggested equipment rental strategies.

A .NET component is an internet service that customers access from a variety of manners including web browsers and spreadsheets. BPM and Business Rules software enables the publication of these web services. By publishing the web service, your customers and trading partners easily incorporate them into your internet services. This is known as 'exposing' the web service to the public.

Another challenge facing Sumter is how to cut the cost of coordinating equipment delivery. When equipment is not available locally, it is sent from the nearest location. A clerical team prints out all the delivery orders for the current week and posts them on a magnetic board. They visually inspect the board for bottlenecks and try to remove them. This process creates volatile delivery costs. Because the process is error prone, Sumter's management wants an automated solution.

The CEO aims to expand contract maintenance of contractor owned equipment. A services oriented system would expand the maintenance offerings to other organizations. The powers of SAP PM could be exposed as another web service. When a contractor subscribes to the service, he would use another .NET or web service application to post the utilization hours to Sumter's SAP PM system, and the business process would push the maintenance repair orders. The SAP PM web service should first be built for internal use so that it meets the needs of the regional offices. Sumter personnel include trained maintenance crews, yet they are not getting all the work orders.

2.1.3 Sumter's Business Strategy and the SOA

Sumter's business strategy is a good example of the use of an economic sector's composite information chain. In the construction industry, this chain flows from project design to competitive bidding to contract award to construction and finally inspection. Sumter connects to the chain with data for bidding and equipment and labor for construction.

The service oriented architecture is a combination of technology and design approaches that allow a company to combine their business processes with customers and vendors in the economy.

The strategy has two core strengths: lower cost of equipment, and the ability to maintain that equipment. OEM partnerships allow Sumter to buy the equipment in bulk at a lower price. Their maintenance skills allow them to offer leases at a lower price. They again lower the cost by selling the used equipment to near and offshore sources. Contractor's capital should naturally seek this efficiency. Because Sumter publishes these services on the internet, their business process positions these strengths in the construction industry.

A Process for Developing the Business Architecture

Figure 2.1 presents a business process for the business architecture activity of the BPM/BR Method. The process first develops business model and continues to develop business cases for projects that align the needs gaps of the enterprise.

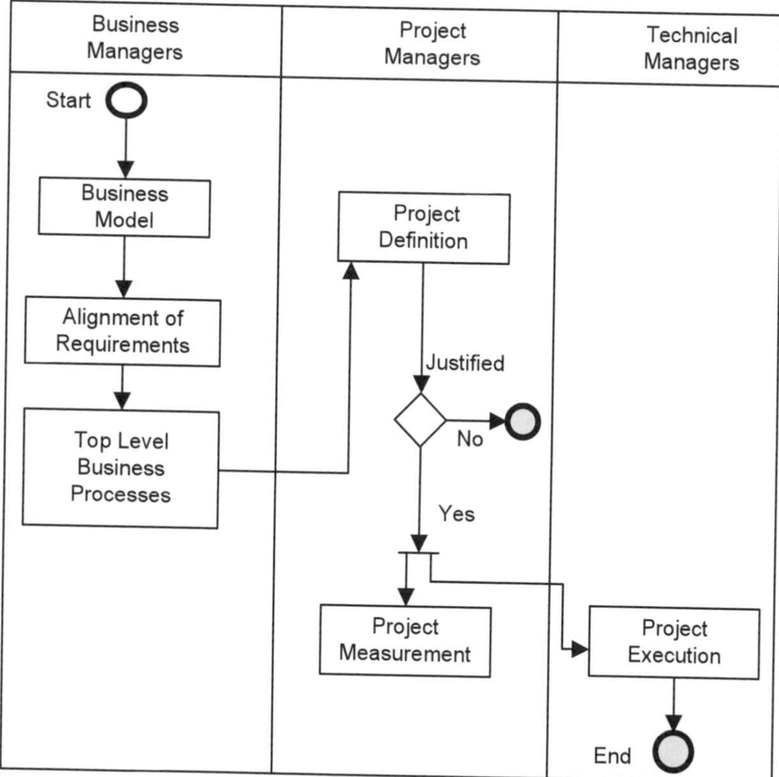

Figure 2.1 A Business Process for business architecture develops a project portfolio that aligns business strategy gaps with projects.

Concept Diagram for Business Architecture

Figure 2.2 presents a diagram of the concepts of the business architecture process. Figure 2.2 is not a data model; it outlines the topics, software, output and information flowing through the activities of the business architecture process. The idea shows the alignment activity creates candidates for BPM projects. The staff should justify each project candidate with a business case, priority, scope definition and time frame. Several projects may affect several business processes. After the process, the technical team does the selected projects in the following processes of the BPM.

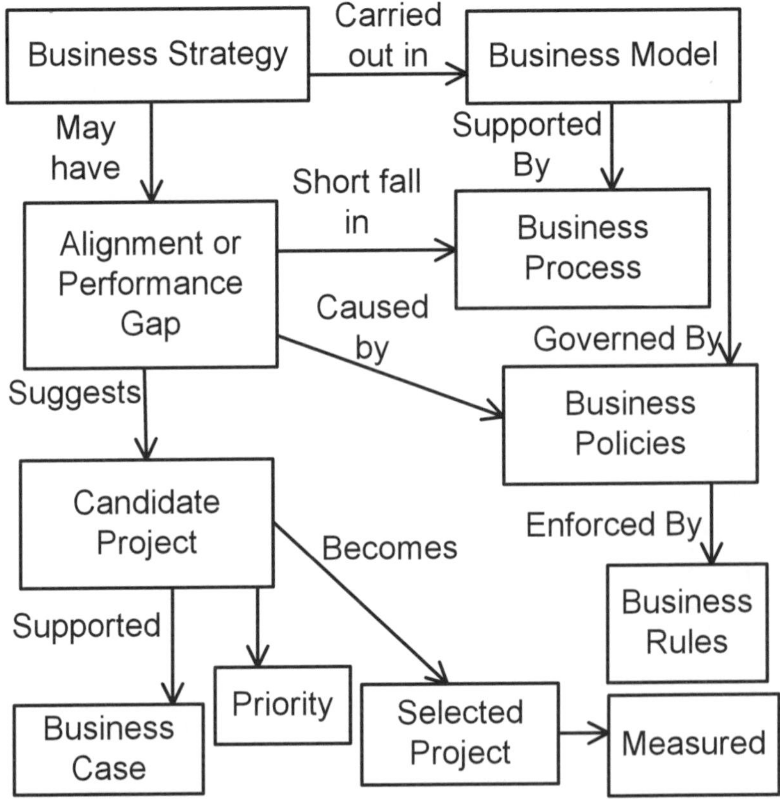

Figure 2.2 The Business Process for business architecture utilizes this concept schema to perform its work.

A business model is carried out by business processes. Business processes are governed by business policies that should be enforced by business rules.

A performance gap or strategy/capability alignment problem should be corrected with new or adjusted processes and policies.

After most business processes, I am going to present a concept diagram. These diagrams will logically describe the types of data that activities use in the preceding process diagram. By taking this approach I hope to avoid the technical tedium of entity relation diagrams or object hierarchies. Nonetheless a capable data modeler should be able to convert a concept diagram into a data model.

Sumter's Business Architecture

Obviously, I can not present every aspect of Sumter Rent's business architecture. Consider the challenges that this company faces. Sumter executive management plans to tackle the CEO's strategic goals for the business in a way that will meet these objectives:

- Expand the customer's online self-service: accept reservations, add corporate discounts, tell customers of available equipment.
- Reduce maintenance costs by improving the business process of using SAP PM, position the business process as a customer service.
- Offer equipment operators from a trading partner to customers.
- Balance inventory against projected demand and resell the aging inventory at the ideal time and price.

Since they want collaboration with customers and trading partners, these objectives are only practicable with a composite application. We will need Business Intelligence for the last requirement. When we tackle these goals, we'll see that Sumter's executive management will need to direct the strategies and objectives within the contexts of the business. Because IT plays such a big role, the technical team's project cycles provide systems integration for this vision.

Sumter executives have appointed an IT management team that has the authority to initiate, monitor and control the projects that are decided. The activities of business architecture become the first step for improving and modernizing the business infrastructure.

Aligning Business Strategies with Systems in a Service Oriented Approach

Sumter Rents' business model aims to align the parts of their existing process model to meet the goals and challenges that I have discussed. Success will give Sumter Rents the most competitive business practices in the rental industry. The practice has changed from the customer service model for the equipment rental business. First, there has been consolidation of small equipment rental companies. This consolidation has lowered prices and increased offering variety. Next, the internet service model simplified shopping for equipment. Now, businesses expectations in a service oriented economy and the internet also change the competitive model. The .NET "rental process" worksheet I described is a competitive practice. Another competitive practice is combining SAP PM Software power with Sumter's maintenance abilities.

The BPM movement is already changing many of Sumter Rent's commercial practices. For instance, BPM has affected Sumter rents relations with customers in the areas of retail and finance. Sumter's trading partners include manufacturing, service industries, insurance and increasingly Sumter utilizes services that are offered on the internet. For instance: Sumter sees their supplier's order's delivery schedule through the internet. Sumter Rents has outsourced customer's credit references to companies. Sumter uses a number of products which have off shored customer support.

As well as specific vertical business practices, consider the universal practices for accounting, logistics, planning, economic data gathering, and human resources. My point is that any special competence or competitive advantage can be exposed with a service for others to use. We see this in Sumter Rents' plan to combine equipment and labor into one source. Sumter's hope is that their competitive advantage will grow along with their expanded service offerings.

Since Sumter's management has decided to evaluate new business processes in maintenance and a new product line - contract maintenance - the managers should perform some 'gap' analysis. In the 'gap' analysis, the Sumter IT management team decides the needs of the organization and then evaluates these against the current IT environment. The purpose is to evaluate, qualify and quantify the difference between the systems they have and the ones they need. The Sumter IT management team inventories the building blocks of the organization's activities and then contrasts that set of activities with the current IT environment. For example, Sumter wants to replace their manual scheduling system. Sumter management will need to evaluate logistical software such as Manugistics or others.

Sumter's Basic Business Model

Business architectures classify the types of core interactions that manage the units of work of the organization, including buy-side types (such as ordering, replenishment) and sell-side types (such as offerings, contracting, salvage). There might be others, such as taxes or financial transactions. For Sumter, the classifications are:

- Buy Side: Buy Equipment, Order Spare parts, and Pass-through labor.
- Sell Side: Customer Equipment Leases, Customer Labor, Used Equipment Sales.

Next, the management team develops a simple top-level diagram of Sumter's business process. Then they map it to the supporting systems. The purpose of this mapping is to develop project plans.

At this early stage, Sumter management needs to decide if the business needs to replace one more of the legacy practices or systems with commercial software. If not, the technical team should build interfaces to the legacy system, publish them as web services, and control them with business processes.

Sumter is going to phase their old maintenance management process into a part of a composite application. Here, the integration software will "gate" the processes to the legacy system. Gating a system in a composite application allows the old systems to be gradually phased out. This phase-out could occur by division or geographic region. This strategy times the enterprise addition of the commercial software application. We hope it also reduces the concerns the organization may have about the cost of integration.

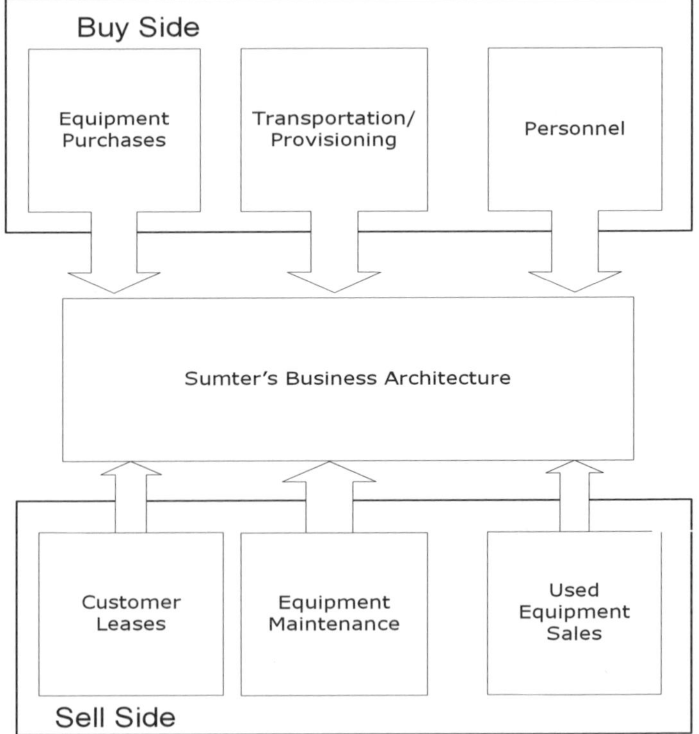

Figure 2.3 This diagram depicts Sumter's core activities. The project portfolio is developed from these activities.

Figure 2.3 presents the core activities for the CEO's goal: to expand Sumter Rents into the top 3 marketplace leaders by developing a closer relationship with key customers. The project areas are summarized in table 1.

Business Area	Support System	Needed Alignment
Equipment Purchases	SAP Inventory	Business Intelligence
Order Provisioning	Manual Scheduling	Comprehensive Automated Logistics
Equipment Maintenance	SAP PM	Composite Web enabled application, service for posting equipment usage hours
Customer Leases	Sumter Customer Portal	Quotations for Contracts, Notifications, CRM suggestions
Used Equipment Sales, balance inventory to demand	AD-Hoc as requested by buyers agents	Business Intelligence

Table 2.1 The business area and the alignments needed to meet the aims of Sumter Management.

After Sumter's management team completes a simple gap analysis, they define a simple model of the business process that a particular project should provide. In the BPM/BR approach, business processes are independent of the systems and individual organizations that execute them, so the team builds a transition to the best solution even if the current systems cannot support the ideal business objective. The kinds of elements the team should explore in the ideal model should include the following:

- identification of opportunities of process realignment,
- out sourcing,
- modernizations of activities, and
- tuning the results of mergers and reorganization.

The management team realized that the initial purchase of construction equipment is connected to the sales of aged equipment. Orders of new equipment should be matched with projected orders for leases for the time that Sumter Rents owns the equipment. The technical team realized that they should consolidate the entire process into a Business Intelligence capability.

If your enterprise wants to initiate a BPM/BR, you will need to follow a clear and strategic method. Developing and completing a small pilot project with simple, achievable goals, and one or two limited services is often a good way to get started. For instance, you might publish some important data for your clients to use. You might automate some legacy data processing functions with BPM (chapter 7). If you build some high-level business process diagrams, as I will do next, you might identify a possible pilot project. A pilot would allow you to test out the BPM/BR and see the results it provides before you fully commit to it. The business process diagrams should describe an area that has been targeted for improvement, upgrade or alignment with goals. The pilot program may involve integrating one new software application, building a user application, or improving process management. One very important aspect of the pilot program is that it involves business and technical personnel.

Building Top Level Business Process Diagrams

Sumter Rents' managers have met, and they have developed a high-level business process for the customer and equipment parts of their business. As I mentioned earlier, developing a draft business process diagram (BPD) is a bit like whiteboard brainstorming. A BPD is not a "process flow" diagram. It is a representation of a long running transaction (LRT). The shift from process flow to LRT is a critical idea in composite applications. Your programs provide the services that activities need to run. BPM design software manages the details and activity. The runtime calls them at the right moment. Think of each piece of rental equipment as a transaction that starts when the equipment enters their store inventory and is finished when it is sold, salvaged or destroyed. Because it could be years before it is finished, this is a long running transaction.

Figure 2.4 presents the central process for Sumter Rents: the equipment process. This process depicts equipment in the system as a long running transaction. It starts when equipment enters the inventory and ends when the equipment is either sold or leased. After equipment is entered into the inventory, it is entered in SAP PM if it has a maintenance schedule. (SAP PM does not manage some items, such as hand tools and road barriers.) After the staff checks in the equipment, they assign the equipment to a retail store. Now it is available for lease. At Sumter Rents' retail locations, the equipment cycles through customer leasing and maintenance. It leaves the loop when the equipment either reaches its salvage age or Sumter Rents decides to sell it.

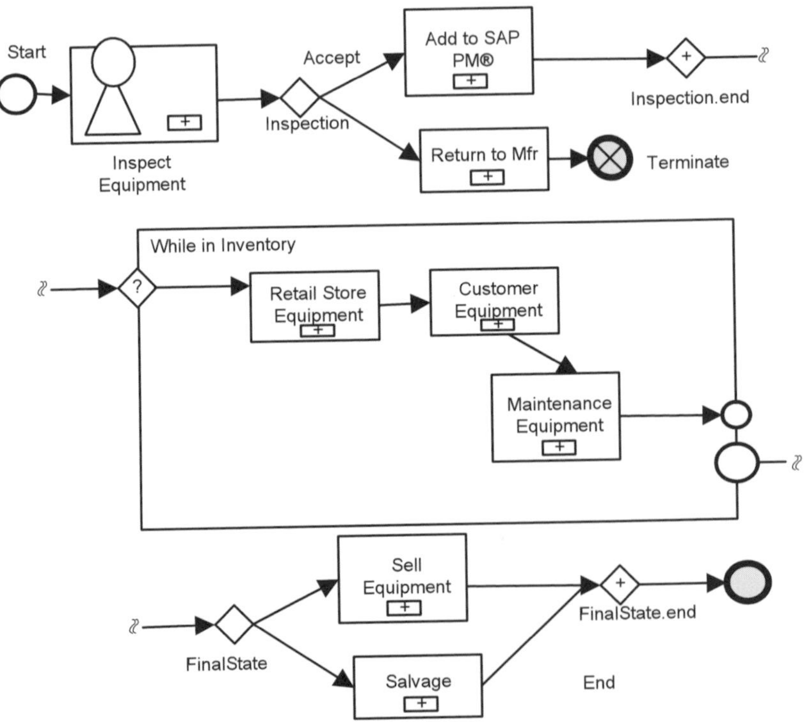

Figure 2.4 The equipment business process.

Let me explain the diagram a bit. Each business process diagram has a start (○▷) and an end (▷○). Activities are shown as boxes. Activities can be programs, web services or subprocesses. The lines denote the flow of information between the activities. Decisions are denoted with pointy boxes (◇), while loops are shown as boxes and have a ◇-symbol on the left hand side. There are more notations to be covered in the chapter on Business Process Management. These notations are similar to other business process modeling standards that have been developed.

Because BPM software coordinates the activities, the business process approach simplifies the creation of applications. The programming team works with the code that performs the activities, and coordination is managed by the BPM software.

When I develop management-level abstract diagrams, I assume that every major activity is a subprocess. These are denoted with the (⊞) boxes in the lower half of the diagram. This way, I develop a list of business processes that must be completed in the business process modeling phase of the task.

The BPD show on Figure 2.4 has sufficient detail for project planning. There are three important subprocesses that will need to be completed to meet our goals:

- Check Equipment into Store Inventory.
- Check the maintenance status of the equipment in SAP PM.
- Lease the equipment to customers.

Traditionally, most IT groups build separate customer applications and equipment applications. Even if they use a unified data model, the IT group writes code that orchestrates the two applications. With BPM, we discover the long term business processes and we build a business process diagram that runs. This is a better model of our business as it reduces the need to coordinate separate applications.

A Project Management Approach in a Six Sigma Organization

Sumter's business management team defines its priorities by utilizing the six-sigma method as the one shown in Figure 2.5. This method identifies and prioritizes the short-term business problems that have clear benefits. These benefits might improve the productivity of organizations, as in the transportation logistics or relationships with customer.

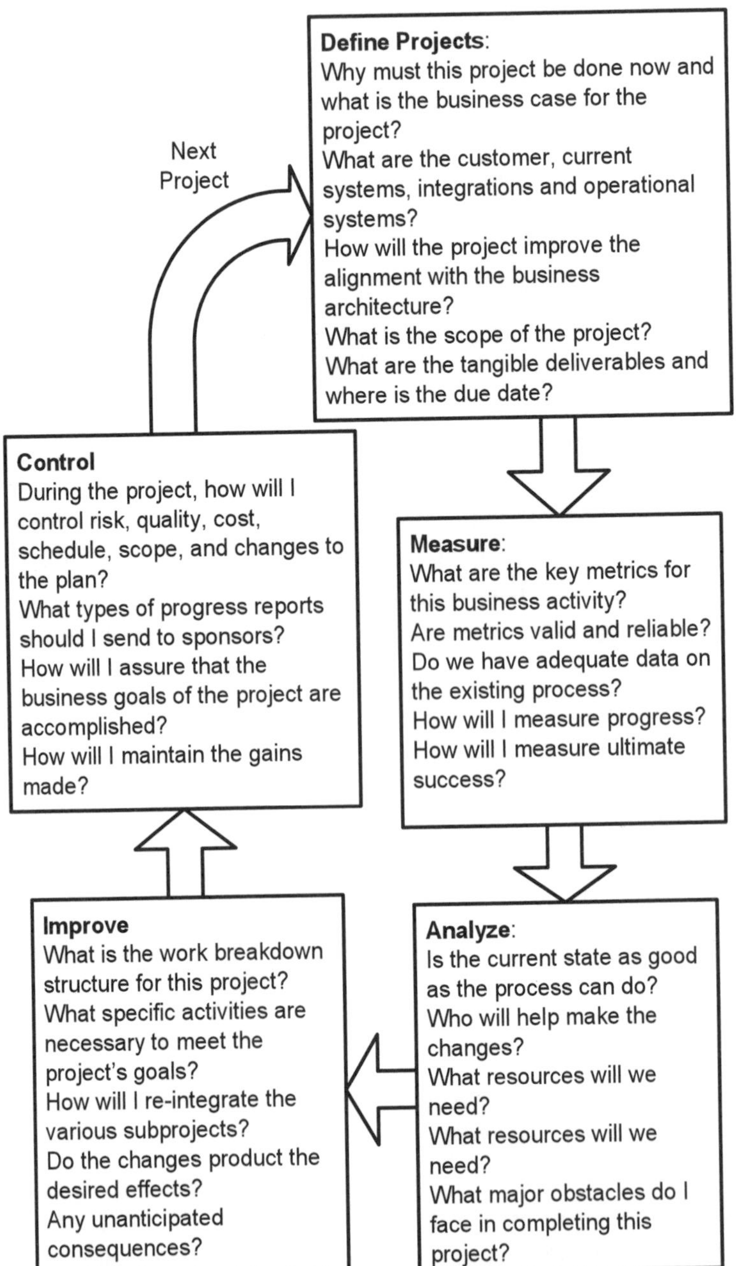

Figure 2.5 For Sumter's Six-Sigma methodology, the business architecture activity is where the scope of the project is determined (Copyright © 2003 by Thomas Pyzdek).

Project Definition for the Portfolio

In project definition, our management team selects projects that align business strategy with the present or future IT environment. During this step, they build a case for why a particular project should be done. To select a project, they define the problems and issues that they want to solve in the BPM/BR project portfolio. It might take many projects to modernize the entire architecture, yet each project should benefit the business. Earlier, we discussed the business architecture and decided the areas that needed alignment. This identified where to start. Now, we want to be more specific in defining the project.

Our team details the areas of business that need to be improved, as well as the areas that are helped with a better IT system. The questions they ask include: What are the business issues? What are the issues that remain from the current architecture? How can they be improved and made more efficient? Should a system be cut out?

For Sumter Rents, I will state the project definitions and tasks as follows:

Customer Lease Selection Improvements The Six-Sigma processes definition bullets include:

- Why is the project needed now? To provide the competitive levels of service to the largest customers, Sumter Rents needs to improve its web-based customer service. Anecdotal evidence suggests that the company is losing income when customers would actually wait another few days for equipment from Sumter.
- Highlights of the business case? We covered the key parts of the business case for the lease improvements earlier. Key economic drivers include an increasing use of heavy equipment leases by construction companies. The risk to the company is that they will lose sales volume to the competition with better customer support models.
- The target customer is the construction contractor. However, any group needing short to medium term leases will benefit from these improvements.
- The current web system will need to be adjusted. The IT team will need to use the BPM software to connect the customer orders to SAP order entry. Several .NET parts will be needed.

- The proposed project combines an improved customer support model and a .NET process spreadsheet. By creating a composite application that combines customer orders and project planning, the project will align with the business architecture.
- The scope of the project is as follows: Sumter will develop a process for enrolling customers into a preferred group. The preferred group will be given access to special corporate discounts. They will receive a .NET spreadsheet that enables them to calculate the cost of the equipment leases in their project costs. The special web services will also allow them to secure quotations for equipment operators. In addition, if the wanted equipment is unavailable, the application will notify them when it is in a store near them.
- The tangible deliverables for the customer service improvements are: a new web storefront, a web-based process for customers to apply for preferred partner status and .NET services to publish pricing and availability.
- Sumter Management expects the project team to complete the project in three quarters.

Internal Maintenance Management Process Users access the SAP PM module through the thick client. SAP offers an iDOC to allow the state of the equipment to be posted as a web service. When equipment is either checked in or at a predefined time interval, the software automatically reviews the maintenance status of the equipment. The Six-Sigma process definition bullets include:

- There are two drivers for the immediacy of the maintenance management process improvement. First, every organization does not use SAP PM. This is especially true of the recently acquired stores. The result is that equipment is not always maintained according to the manufacturer's recommendations. Second, the manual process of entering data that triggers maintenance is error prone. The SAP PM system produces a few wrong maintenance orders. The result of the mistaken orders is wasted clerical labor.
- Highlights of business case: Equipment rental is the primary revenue generator for Sumter Rents. Because equipment is the largest capital expense, efficient and effective maintenance is one of the critical roles of Sumter Rents. Further, the value

of the aftermarket sales of equipment is strengthened by an aggressive maintenance regime. The purpose of this process is to improve and simplify this critical role. Currently, Sumter Rents is achieving a 93% compliance with the manufacturers recommended maintenance schedule. The aim of the process improvement is to raise this to better than 99%. The long-term benefit to this project is an improved process that can be simultaneously published to Sumter's customers. It is hoped that the web-based service will be a discriminator for customers. The benefit of the equipment maintenance contract is that the project will create revenue.

- The customer of the maintenance process improvements is Sumter Rents' equipment managers. After the process has been proven, it will be part of the maintenance service contracts.
- The current systems are the SAP PM and the Sumter Rents portal.
- Equipment is the centerpiece of Sumter Rents' business. Sumter Rents is skilled in equipment maintenance. The project improves the alignment with the business architecture by improving the maintenance service of equipment.
- The scope of this project is limited to automated maintenance scheduling in SAP PM.
- There are two deliverables in the scope of this project. The first is an internet form to post equipment odometer readings to SAP PM. The second is a program that pushes orders for maintenance automatically to equipment managers.
- The management expects the team to complete this project in six months.

Balance Inventory and Used equipment sales

- The executive management aims to sell the optimum amount of used equipment while keeping a profitable inventory of modern equipment. The current system is not as disciplined as it should be.
- Highlights of the business case: Sales of used equipment are an important source of income and a mechanism for financing the modernization of Sumter Rents' fleet. Because deciding the quantities of equipment to sell is complex, Sumter Rents is risking poor decisions in the used sales volumes and

a less than optimal turnover in the inventory. The risk in the current process is unknown—the sales of used construction equipment might be better managed for more capital.

- The customer of this project is the chief financial officer of Sumter Rents.
- The system will need to need to build sales projections for the year. The system will need to gather data from some external sources. The project team will need to build interfaces with new equipment costs from manufacturers.
- There are no commercially available solutions for this problem. However, native capabilities of Business Intelligence tools, including "dash boards" and business activity monitoring, play a role in this application.
- This project aims to increase the quality of the inventory. It does so by balancing the used equipment sales with projected business revenue. The project improves the alignment with the business architecture.
- The scope of this project is limited to decision support for the equipment sales problem.
- The tangible deliverable is a construction of a Business Intelligence solution.
- The management expects the team to complete this project in six months.

As a project is started, the management team performs project management. A selected project becomes part of a project portfolio that is monitored and fine tuned.

Measure. As a BPM/BR project progresses, the management team monitors the progress. Software projects are often measured in terms of function points, and these are usually very technical. The ultimate success of the BPM/BR project happens after the technical work is complete, and metrics that drive the business change.

The benefits of these three projects should yield tangible increase in business performance metrics. The customer process improvement should increase rental sales to construction customers. The customer process will be built with measurements of the number of follow-on sales that occur after a customer is notified that his needed equipment is available. SAP PM monitors the compliance with manufactures maintenance regimens. An improvement in the maintenance function should improve this metric. Lastly, Business Intelligence in the equipment sales areas should improve the revenue of the operation.

Analyze. As the project proceeds, its status should be analyzed for the quality of its progress. When management closely monitors the quality of the project, they avoid potential failures and obstacles to success.

Improve Over time. The managers view the projects in aggregate and they may merge portions of the projects.

Control. The project sponsor controls the risks, quality, cost schedule and changes to the program. These activities are the chief business architecture tools that move the enterprise into alignment with its goals.

Finally, security is an increasingly key consideration in the business architecture of the enterprise. Business security should consider the sensitivity of operations and data. The enterprise must protect its data assets and intellectual property. Increasingly, government and customer relationships mandate a model for protecting data privacy.

The outputs of the business architecture include the structure of the business processes that the organization is working towards, independent of the existing systems and practices. This architecture is an ideal that the organization is striving for. The BPM/BR creates systems that are characterized by a loose coupling of the business process and the systems that support it. From this ideal, projects are selected that implement the corporate vision. Other outputs of this activity are the selected projects, business cases for the projects and a set of tasks and deliverables. During this activity, each of the projects is monitored as a portfolio.

Business Architecture Discussion

The first activity of the BPM/BR is the business architecture. Here is where we explore and discover new initiatives for services to be published and used. Where is the business in the information chain? What are the areas of the business that should be outsourced to more efficient areas? In this activity, the BPM/BR addresses the strategic and tactical goals of the business. This should be old hat for business executives, but what is new is the application of BPM to reengineer their processes for competitive reasons. Business architecture in the BPM/BR provides a new type of systems integration for the strategies and objectives of management. The outcome of the business architecture is a portfolio of projects that should obliterate the IT/Business divide.

Executive managers understand that information systems are a critical supporting part of every modern business strategy. They direct and support these systems with an eye on the value of corporate investment in technology. The BPM/BR process provides this value these ways:

- Raising the complexity and scope of the problems that are tackled by merging of business processes and business rules,
- Publishing the native capabilities in an innovative way will raise an organization's agility,
- Easily tuning and configuring processes, cutting the time needed to change a business rule or process.

Many types of changes that formerly needed programming are cut. Because of BPM/BR's focus on Business Intelligence, managers have ready access to the critical information they need.

A strategic goal of most corporate management models is to align the best, or most profitable, business practices with the process model. Some of these new practices need complex, atomic decisions about data. For instance, customers essentially create their own rules and processes in CRM. Highly sophisticated international transactions need sophisticated models for developing currency factors. Predicting the failure of systems needs the wholesale application of data mining techniques against large volumes of data. These complexities often need tuning.

More often your organization solves problems by tuning metrics and key performance indicators. These are tactical things. At this level, you are measuring what is looming, what are we doing well, what are we, how can we get more out of the business, what type cross-selling can we do? How can we improve the % of our target customer?

Either strategically or tactically, management leadership sets goals and objectives that should be measured over time or in milestones. Executive level planning like this often leads to changes in the supporting business systems:

a business activity is outsourced, a new offering made to customers, or trading partners added. This is where BPM/BR fits in. It will develop projects that support these goals and objectives.

The BPM/BR supports many of these new integration needs. Some business architecture initiatives that might affect business systems at the process level include:

- Improved understanding of customer behavior.
- Providing managers with better support systems.
- Cutting the cost of purchasing; bundling purchase agreements.
- Outsourcing operations such as human resources, customer finance, shipping, or manufacturing.
- Changing financial practices such as payment on receipt of materials.
- Putting into effect government mandated regulations including mandated disclosures, environmental and health and safety regulations.
- Better intelligence on real-time data, predictive failures, data mining, occult patterns that change yet yield informed decisions

BPM/BR projects are an outgrowth of the basic planning of the initiatives that it takes to meet these goals.

I look at business architecture as the building blocks that create and support the success of the organization. Components might range from the abstract, such as the capability to foresee business opportunities, to the concrete such as manufacturing capability. The composite of these form a business' most detailed strategy. These building blocks are linked and supported by streams of information. Adding a new block to the stack always influences communications and often needs the type of enterprise application integration (EAI) that is supported by the BPM/BR.

In the BPM/BR, the first part of the business architecture activity is for the BPM/BR management team to inventory the building blocks of the organization's activities and then contrast the activities with the current IT environment. This is limited to the building blocks that surround an initiative. Parts of the resources of the business are the large scale systems such as ERP, Human Resources, Logistics, and others.

From this first sketch of the problem, and the areas that it touches, the BPM/BR team should define an abstract or a virtual model of the business process that a project - or groups of projects - should provide. As with the

Business Process Management concept, the BPM/BR business architecture strives for an ideal model of business processes, one that is independent of the systems that are operating the business. The aim of the analysis part of the business architecture is to define a project that aligns business strategy with the present, or future, IT environment.

Chief officer level initiatives often create portfolios of projects needed to create the result. Portfolios might be managed vertically, assigned to areas of finance, engineering or IT, or horizontally by objectives.

In summary, it is important in your project definition for you to write a business case for the project. In finalizing the project plans, the team should outline the current systems involved—the integration elements, operational systems and analytical or data warehouses. If the project requires the upgrade or substantial retrofit of a legacy system, the BPM/BR team should determine whether a commercially available (COTS) solution is available.

When COTS is available, then an independent return on investment (ROI) analysis should be developed.

Armed with a business case and ROI, the team will have an objective case for how the project improves the alignment with the business architecture. After they select a project, they develop the scope, tangible deliverables and due date for the project. A project sponsor is a team member or members that are responsible for the completion of the project. This is not, however, the end of their involvement in the subsequent activities.

The service oriented business architecture (SOA) strives for an ideal model of business processes; one that is independent of the systems that are currently operating the business. The SOA evolves over time. With an SOA approach, organizations expose small portions of the current system architecture as a service and move towards the target business architecture.

Summary

- Business architecture describes the basic building blocks of an enterprise, including strategies, tactics and the infrastructure to be built.
- You use business processes to align tactics and strategies with the organization and technical infrastructure. The high-level business processes become candidates for project definition.

- In project definition, you clarify the need and set up the scope, deliverables and time frames for the project.
- We defined three projects in our case study. These are:

1. Create an improved equipment maintenance process. The purpose of this project is to simplify maintenance of equipment with SAP PM. The improved process will be offered to customers as a service.
2. Create a closer relation with commercial customers by improving their rental experience and simplifying the chore of estimating construction project details.
3. Create a more precise method for deciding what quantity of equipment to sell on the open market. This method will use Business Intelligence technology.

References

Karmarkar , Uday, 2004. "Will You Survive the Services Revolution?
" Boston, MA, Harvard Business Review.

CHAPTER THREE

Business Process Management

When a customer fills out an order for something on a website, he has completed only one process step from the view of the business. The enterprise has not done its work with the order until the business rules approves the customer, the order entry system supplies the order, the ERP's accounts payable module is called, and perhaps a work flow system sends an email. In BPM jargon this is known as a long running transaction (LRT). In a Business Process Management approach these steps are activities. Different organizations and different systems complete the LRT. For instance, the company with the web site may have outsourced some steps. Someone has to ship the box, so some steps are manual. Each system that performs the computer work of the process is one activity or unit of work.

You and your team should start to develop a project's business processes by setting up its objectives. Building this is a progression from the objectives to the sequence of activity steps. This will build what I call the Core Business Process (CBP). The CBP is independent of the COTS applications that perform accounting and other roles.

The questions the team should ask itself are: What is the scope of the process? What are the steps that the process must finish in order for the business to reach its goal? Next, the analysts define what data the LRT should gather and how it will provide this data to the specific systems that need it. You develop this by cataloging the data and services needed by the systems and mapping this to the core process activities and data.

The Business Rules Approach becomes important where the processes start to enforce policies. Business rules need to convert, manipulate or corroborate the data. The most common examples are decisions about the validity of the data that is entering an activity in the process. If a user has not correctly entered a form or transaction, then the process must return an error to the requester. If the business process branches to manage subprocesses, then the rules might decide this. I am going to describe where you place the business rules into an activity on the diagram. The activity will then be linked to a web service for the business rules need of the activity. The benefit of the composite process occurs when these business rules change. For instance, if you change a decision that accepts or rejects data, then the process itself will not need to change.

Our project portfolio aligns Sumter Rents' business systems with strategies for customers and equipment. We aim to build business processes for Sumter Rents that will carry out needed business tactics as long running transactions. They touch many systems, yet, for Sumter Rents, they are the basic transactions of the business.

A business process diagram (BPD) depicts an iteration of a long running transaction. BPM software allows you to oversee the progress of the transaction as it moves through the process. For instance, the equipment process for a bulldozer may endure for years. Earlier, I made the analogy that a business process diagram is similar to a process flow diagram. What is different is the information within the lines between the activities. Each activity has the ability to calculate, assign, or delete downstream data with upstream values. A transaction in a business process is like one sheet from a clipboard of business forms. The process manipulates and stores all the information. The BPD design tools define what actions take place on the data sets. Business model symbols include ingenuous activity types, schedulers, and flow control. Flow control includes switches (*if… then … else*) and others that simplify the control of the data in the business process. Think of the business process diagram as a factory that acts on the business forms in an assembly line process.

I mentioned that business processes are like process flow diagrams; however, they are also atomic, like a single set of related business records. They represent an instance of the business process. Think of my example: the equipment process. The diagram itself applies to the single unit. A bulldozer, a motorized lift—for each of the equipment units that Sumter Rents owns there is an instance of the equipment process. This is the power of the BPEL engine. Obviously, if every piece of equipment has an instance of a business process then you could build queries of the BPEL engine. You could discover *how many units need maintenance today? How many customers have rented bulldozers of type "x" today?*

As your team develops the business process, it should look for areas where policies and data support important decisions. This is where the business rules connect to the process as a service. I suggest that you perform your evaluations with business rules if the process that you are modeling is raising an event or selecting a path in the process flow by:

- Computing conditions across historical data
- Sorting and classifying a process based on numeric causes
- Querying an operational data store for historical events

If you have connected your business process with a service that invokes the rule, then you can easily change the basis for the decision or event.

Business Rules Work Within Business Processes

The choice of what should become a business rule, and what should become a part of the process is not difficult. Consider my earlier statement that business rules mediate the data's content. The business rules should use data to support its decision, and the process should direct that data to the services which consume it or provide other data. Table 3.1 presents some general guidelines for what to carry out as business rules and what to include in the process.

Design Item	Example	Process or Rule
Decision	If customer is preferred then develop greatest discount	Business Rule
Policy	Equipment is sent to maintenance under certain conditions	Business Rule
Post to Application service	SAP PM	Business Process
State, duration, or location of entity	Equipment in maintenance, assigned to customer or at retail store	Business Process
Direct data to branch of process	decisions, while loop, subprocess	Business Process
Read external transaction	Customer equipment on maintenance contract	Business Process
Certify external transaction	Confirm attributes of a transaction	Business Rule
Report data errors to external system	Errors in business rule approval	Business Process
Reference Data	Customer's credit limit	*Business Rule or Business Process
Convert Process data to Interface	Mapping accounting transactions for ERP	*Business Rule or Business Process
Store data in operational data store	Record the clerical details of an Order	*Business Rule or Business Process

Table 3.1 This table lists some guidelines for what should be a part of the business process and what should be a part of the business rules repository.

The business process diagram is often a complex map of flow control. It will have many subprocesses, decisions and *while loops*. Wherever a decision or while loop appears, you should consider the basis for the change in flow.

The business rules should evaluate the data provided by the process. Next, the business rule should provide control to the process so it can make a decision. This is the best use of business rules in the business process.

The last three examples are gray areas. If there are changing means of gaining reference data for a process, and it provides important process parameters for decisions, then you should consider this a business rule. If the reference data are information which the process needs for sequencing or scheduling data, then you might not need the Business Rules Approach. Mapping process parameters into the data needed by an interface is another requirement you might design as a business rule. Business rules are an effective way of managing data when there are a lot of changes in the database.

Finally, if systems outside the business process environment need data, then either business rules or process engines store operational data. BPML engines might populate operational data during an instance of a process.

Sumter's New Processes

During business process modeling, a BPM/BR technical/management team creates or tunes a business process model that supports the project's objectives. What are the mental processes of the team members developing business processes and connecting business rules? They use workshops and communication. They interview the best performing and the worst performing actors in the processes. They review documentation and the notes of the managers of the current process. They identify business rules and the process needs for policies or chose with proper flow control.

There are institutional or traditional ways of gathering information. Sumter Rents has reams of paper, cabinets full of files, and databases overflowing with useful information—from management directives to marketing papers to MIS memorandums. Much important information exists here. Yet, business process modeling is different from data modeling. The purpose of data modeling is to develop a model of *what is*. The purpose of business process modeling is to develop a model of *what should be*.

In the past this information gathering led to data models, use-case analysis and other traditional documents. BPM develops a model of the business about the flow of the important steps from the top of the business down to the lowest details of the systems that need to record important transactions.

A Process for Business Process Modeling

Figure 3.1 presents a business process for modeling business processes. Core process areas are those areas which are essential to a business process, yet independent of the systems that service their needs. If the team needs to design or adjust a core business process, they will do that first. If the only change is to an interface, then they create and adjust the interface processes.

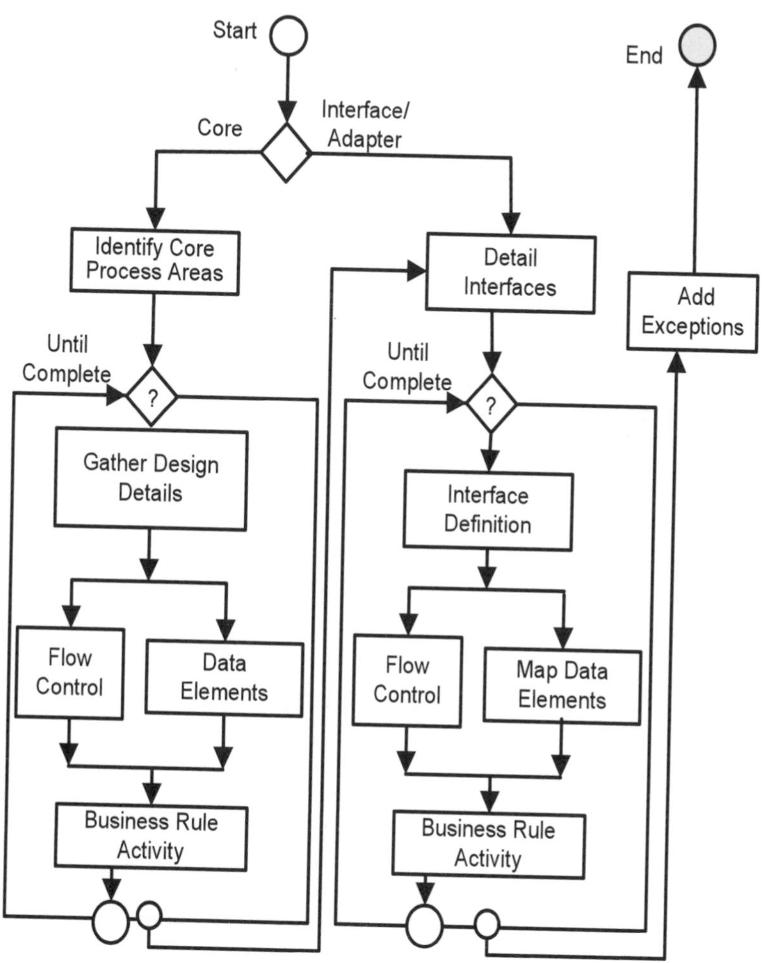

Figure 3.1 The design team creates the Business Process; an iterative process of developing activities connecting them with flow control and mediating the flow with business rules.

I have used a *while loop* to show developing a business process. The next activity is to the gather design details that create a business process design. Design details include use cases for user interfaces or system interfaces. As the team gathers details, they may need to design web screens to collect data. They develop file formats or XML transaction that the business process will read.

Flow controls connect the design details, which become process activities. When the activity needs some external services, it calls a partner application.

After flow controls, the team develops the data—or business entities for the business process. Most business process route an entire business form.

For core business processes and interfaces, the design team will add business rules to the diagram. They evaluate important flow controls to identify subject areas for business rules. Within the process, at the suitable location, the rules carry out policy, constraints or competitive business practices.

In the BPM activity, teams document the workflow of the process steps with BPM software. The process workflow describes the critical path. This includes activities and subprocesses that are run in parallel, or those that are sequential. If the team is working on several business processes, they may need to develop inter-process orchestrations. Afterwards, they might discover opportunities to design a more efficient process.

The final step of the business process is for the project team to define likely exceptions and points of failure. Business processes should be able to recover from reasonable system failures. The project team may need to define compensations, or what to do if the business process must remove a transaction.

The outcome of business process design should be a working process prototype. The prototype corroborates working interfaces and confirms business entities.

A Concept Diagram for the Business Process

Figure 3.2 depicts the concepts of the process shown on Figure 3.1 by connecting the business process and the business rules ideas beneath and within the process definition.

An organization's processes can be classified into Material Processes, Information Processes, and Business Processes. A material process is the assembly or delivery of physical products. Information processes outline the automated, and partly automated, tasks that create, manage, and provide information. A business processes is a market centered description of an organization's activities. A business uses business rules to create policies, guidelines, negotiations and offerings. This is how the business process is controlled and provided with critical information.

The figure below merges these two methods:

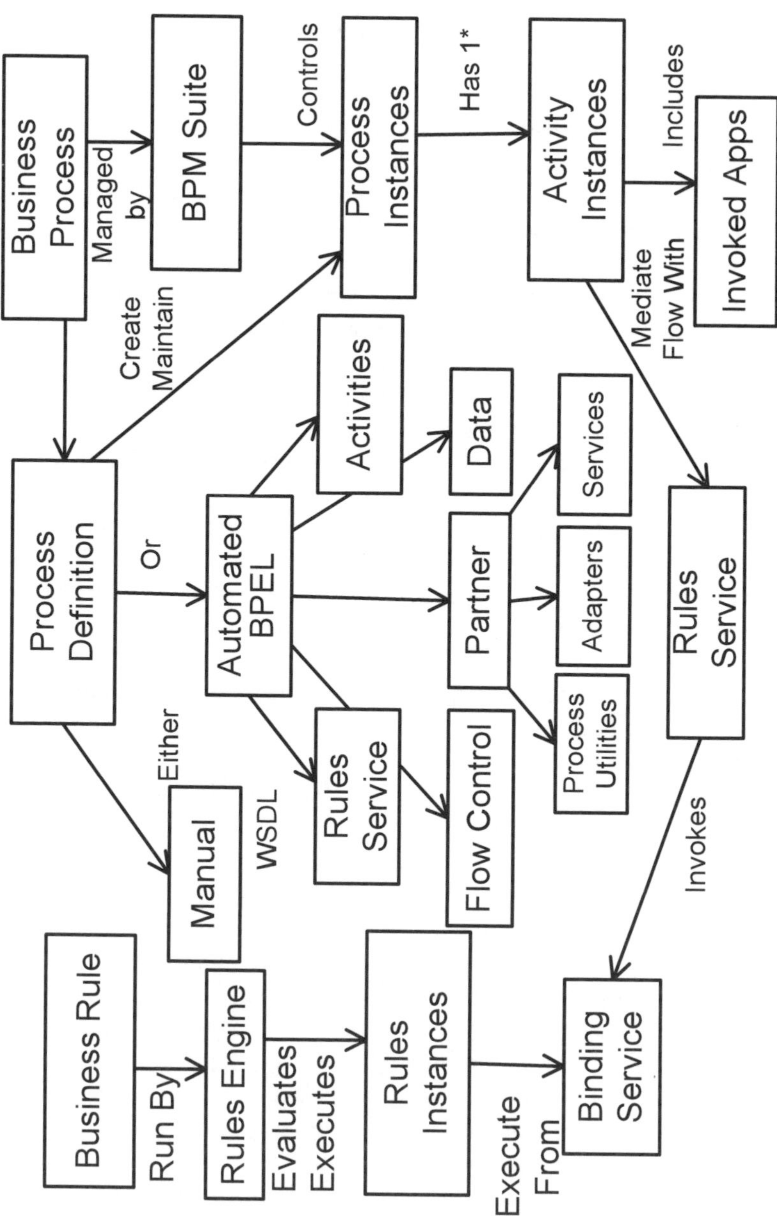

Figure 3.2 A concept decomposition of business rules and business processes with interacting ideas and subject areas. I will describe the specification for the rules service in the next chapter.

The process definition is the centroid of the diagram. The activities in the process description may be fully automated, or may involve humans interacting with computers. Business process modeling language (BPML) models automated processes. Business process execution language (BPEL) directs the detail of the processes, and is arguably the most prevalent way to describe automated business processes. It describes, in a XML specification language, the activities that need to be performed, the participants (partners) who could or should perform them, and the interdependencies that exist among them (flow control). BPEL simplifies describing processes, their tasks, and the dependencies among the tasks. One of these services may be a *rules service,* which is a web service that invokes a call to a business rule.

Prominent BPM software, such as WebMethods™, Tibico™ and SeeBeyond™ provide libraries of services. These services are partners and they are added to your BPEL when you add them to the diagram. Examples of these services are messaging services, file utilities and web user interfaces. BPM software also provides prepackaged services for ERPs. These are known as adapters.

On the right branch of the diagram in Figure 3.2, business processes are managed to completion. BPM software should carry out the BPEL process description; assigning the proper activity to the responsible system or person. For example, the software may assign manual activities and access to the software tools needed to finish the task. These tools might include databases, spreadsheets, and design software. Another role of BPM software is to issue dependencies among the tasks. Finally, the BPM software should support multiple invocations (instances) of a given process and a given task.

Examine the left side of the concept diagram. The business rules engine controls the instances of business rules. By manipulating the rules schema, you control the flow of activities in a business process. A service invoked by the Business Process carries out the business rules. The concept diagram shows this as a *rules service* which is an internal system. In the next chapter I will describe the rules schema which is a part of the business rules repository. The rules schema defines the WSDL that specifies the binding for the business process.

Business processes work with *flows* of data. You might think of these flows as (paper) business forms that move from place to place, person to person. Customer orders or equipment repair tickets are examples. The process is a conduit for one or more of these forms to flow in its designated path. The data comes from outside the business process, either from another system or from a message sent by another business process. The business rule uses the data in the business form to direct the business process. Business rules should correct, certify, and mediate every data item the business uses. Business rules create or encourage special behavior. Separating these two ideas allows an organization to change the decisions without complex changes in computer code.

Scheduling is a critical part of Business Process Management. However, processes drive the business rules that trigger events. For instance, imagine the process that a business needs to *dun* a customer. The business rules should define intensifying processes for contacting a tardy paying customer. We are going to describe a similar requirement for the equipment processes. A process must often check the maintenance schedule to control when the equipment must be serviced. Business rules will decide the criticality of the maintenance when a customer has it.

Lying between the users and operational systems should be the business rules which the enterprise controls; including the stovepipes and the ERP. Special offerings and fine-tuning of the business transactions to increase the yields and offer better customer service is the domain of the business rule. You might even call a CRM system a set of business rules for the individual customer to use. For instance, a rule might set up communications with a customer that would like to rent a particular product. For Sumter Rents, the customer wants to know when equipment is available from a set of locations.

Equipment Maintenance Process Improvements

The equipment process is the most important part of Sumter Rents' business. The process starts with the purchase of equipment, and ends with its sale or disposal. Along the way, customers lease it and the company maintains it with a schedule controlled by SAP PM. We are going to create these processes, and show how BPM software simplifies the steps of gathering the needed data and controls.

Sumter Rent's management has appointed a small team to develop these processes. They gather information from reading standard procedures and visiting equipment managers at stores. Because personnel suggests that the maintenance management is complicated, the team wants to discover the complexity. They hope to find the underlying issues in interviews with the staff.

The design team orally describes the process. In one discussion about the current equipment process, an equipment manager described his view by stating that managers are responsible for four activities:

1. The equipment manager receives and inspects new equipment. If there are inspection issues he is responsible for resolving the issues.
2. The equipment manager prepares the equipment for issue to rental customers.
3. The equipment manager gets the equipment from the customer

after use. He inspects the equipment for damage. He checks the equipment back into rental inventory.

4. The equipment manager is responsible for carrying out scheduled maintenance for the equipment.

This list suggests some starting points for the activities and some decision points and business rules in the business process.

The evidence of a broken process was everywhere..

During the interview, the process team notes that the manager keeps much of his information on clipboards and in notes. In more detailed interviews, they discover that the equipment manager has been running maintenance reports on the store's inventory. The team asks why the manager needs so much data. The managers respond that most equipment maintenance occurs because the hours on the odometer have exceeded a threshold value. There are other conditions that call for maintenance, and the current SAP PM process is only designed for equipment that is on the lot of the retail store, not assigned to a customer.

The questions about the clipboard's data identify several important process issues. With large store inventories, the conditions that cause or trigger preventive maintenance might be unwieldy. Occasionally, the store issues equipment to customers just before the scheduled inventory or a manufacturer recall. For instance: imagine a dangerous defect is discovered in a piece of heavy equipment. Sumter would want to collect this equipment from the customer immediately. When the equipment is off-site for an extended time, the maintenance schedule might lapse. Sometimes Sumter leases equipment to customers without going through the check-in process. So to avoid losing maintenance cycles, the managers keep long printouts of the maintenance schedules of the equipment. An aim of the business process team is to cut these difficulties with a more accurate process.

At this early phase of business process modeling, the team collects basic process and data features of the activities around the project. Important data for the equipment manager includes the equipment identifier and the acceptance date. Manufacturers provide the maintenance regimes, including startup procedures, through SAP PM. The philosophy is a bit different than traditional use-case analysis. BPM's purpose is to discover what *should be* done—it is not to discover what *is* done.

The process team is now able to add more detail to the high-level diagrams which were created in the Business Architecture phase of the project.

As shown in the business process in Figure 3.3, our teams add process activities and decisions after interviewing the equipment manager. I have split the diagram out from top to bottom. The symbol (ℓ) marks a continuity with the process flow from the upper right hand side. You should examine these diagrams and connect the notation on them to the interview discoveries. The equipment inspection might result in a return to the manufacturer for correction or replacement; the team has added a decision to support this. If the local manager accepts the equipment, then SAP PM assigns an equipment identifier to the unit. After the equipment manager has accepted the unit, he might need to perform startup procedures. The business process should immediately call these out.

The process assigns the equipment to store inventory, and the *while loop* starts. Figure 3.3 shows the use of a message queue within the while loop. The *equipment state message* activity:

- Sends the process to the customer sub-process; the customer application has assigned it to a customer
- Sends the process to a retail store: By default, Sumter Rents may move the equipment from store to store
- Sends the process to maintenance if maintenance is warranted
- If Sumter decides to remove the equipment from inventory, then the equipment exits the loop.

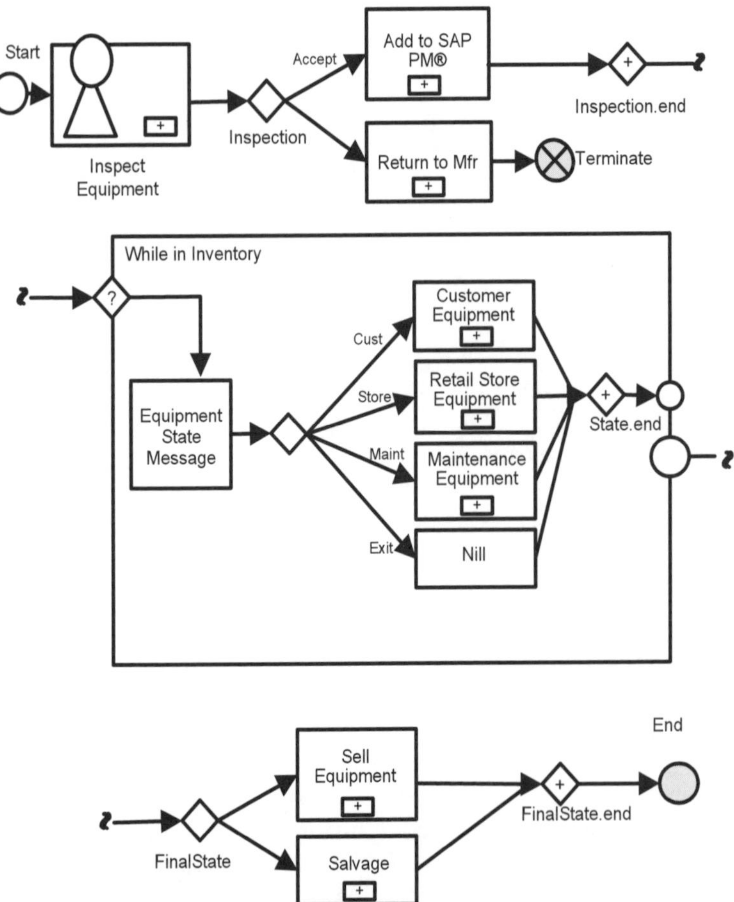

Figure 3.3 This business process diagram depicts a more detailed equipment process. A message queue controls the flow.

On this and future business process diagrams, my aim is to show a portion of what a BPM solution looks like. I have condensed some activities, such as the user activity on the left side of Figure 3.3. In practice, the *inspect equipment activity* would entail more steps than merely hanging a web screen from a business process diagram. A user interface would need some process coordination. The process shown in Figure 3.3 is missing activities that assign values to the data in the process flows.

Conditions continually check for maintenance in the equipment process. This is why we have chosen a message-driven solution to managing the state of the equipment. Messages communicate with all the processes. Five different causes drive the SAP maintenance schedule: age of ownership, equipment hours, manufacturers recall and changing seasons. These causes are independent of where the equipment is in the process—equipment managers cannot depend on the equipment being in the yard in order to perform maintenance. The process needs to respond to these events asynchronously. At any high-level activity, the process should check for a maintenance event. This means that there are different events which call for equipment maintenance: the odometer reading on the unit has reached a certain value, a particular period of time may have passed, a change in the seasons or a manufacturer recall. Since the time based changes occur intermittently, we will need the system to be looking for these events in the background.

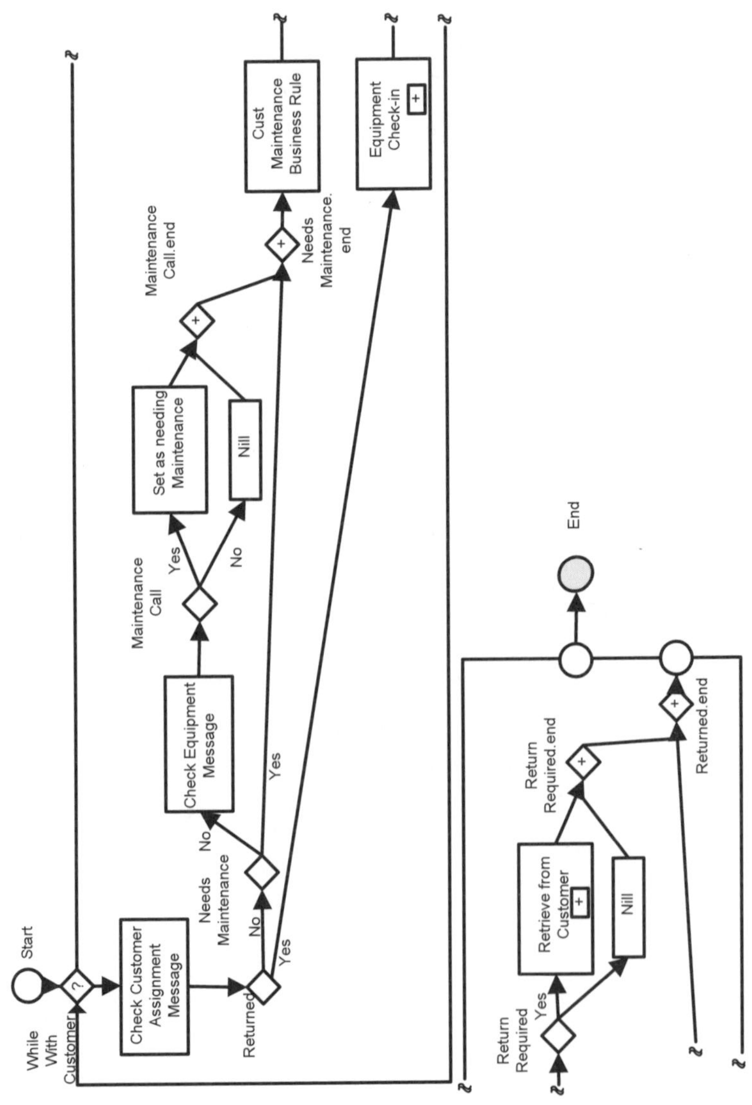

Figure 3.4 This business process diagram depicts the customer assignment subprocess from figure 3.3. It shows how the maintenance events affect the customer assigned equipment.

The *customer equipment* sub-process is presented in figure 3.4. The process continues in a loop until it receives a message that the customer has returned the equipment to a retail store.

In the assigned equipment process, the first activity looks at the message queue for equipment returned by the customer. An application sends the message when the equipment arrives at the retail store. Perhaps a PDA reads a bar code on the equipment. When the equipment has been returned, the process next calls the equipment check-in sub-process which checks for the presence of a maintenance message. If one exists, the process will set the equipment's status as needing maintenance and call the business rule to decide if personnel must bring the equipment into the shop.

Finally, the process returns to the main equipment process. The process will direct the equipment to either the retail store process or the maintenance process.

These processes should be as independent from the means of data entry as possible. This will allow Sumter Rents to develop new ways of entering the data. For instance, at a future date, radio frequency identification (RFID) may perform equipment return. You achieve independence from the method of data collection by using messaging tactics.

Equipment Entities

The purpose of the equipment process is to oversee and control the location of the equipment, and to hold the equipment's data which SAP PM will need in order to decide when maintenance is due. Equipment is either at a retail location, assigned to a customer, or is in maintenance. The service history is a list of the odometer readings and date values for the equipment. Retail stores inspect the equipment when it is received from the customers, or when it is sent from another retail location. The equipment process works with a simple entity, the equipment business entity object. The logical information diagram for this is shown on Figure 3.5.

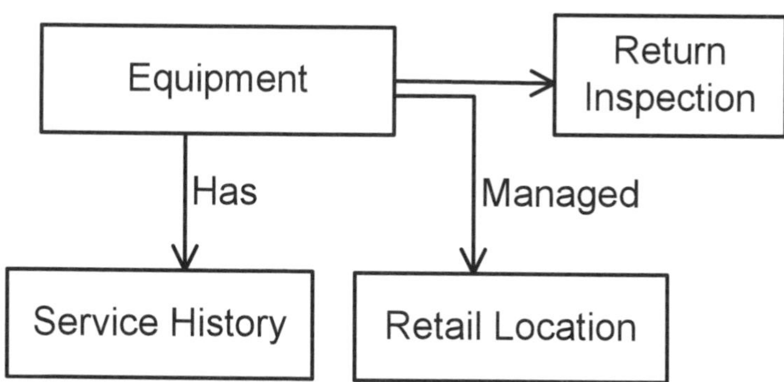

Figure 3.5 The equipment process uses the equipment entity to manage the state and location of a piece of equipment.

To be concise, I have not shown the attributes of the equipment information. The equipment process creates an instance of the equipment form, and its fields, in the first activity in Figure 3.3.

Even though Sumter Rents is using SAP PM, they maintain a separate catalog of equipment in an operational datastore for use across the enterprise. The operational datastore is a database of information that is independent of the commercial applications. The equipment catalog will be useful in other processes and applications, particularly the data warehouse.

Offering Equipment Maintenance Services

The BPM suite enables Sumter Rents to offer the equipment maintenance process to their customers as a product. The process design team has designed an equipment maintenance process that is independent of the larger Sumter Rents equipment process. By exposing the equipment maintenance service as an external process, Sumter Rents can offer this to their customers.

The process team designs the customer's contract service to use SAP PM through the existing maintenance process. It accepts the same data: mileage or hours on the equipment. The top-level of the contract maintenance process is presented in Figure 3.3. The team has designed the different steps for the equipment for the entire life of the customer contract.

In the first step, a separate application enters the customer's equipment into SAP PM. There is a customer contract and billing process and the equipment only exists for the life of the contract. The process may also renew a customer's contract.

After the process enters a customer's contracted equipment, the service part of the process loop may begin. The process in Figure 3.6 depends on a message that it receives from a process looking at equipment in SAP PM. For instance, if the maintenance department must lubricate the equipment every six months, this business process will notify the customer and the service manager of this need.

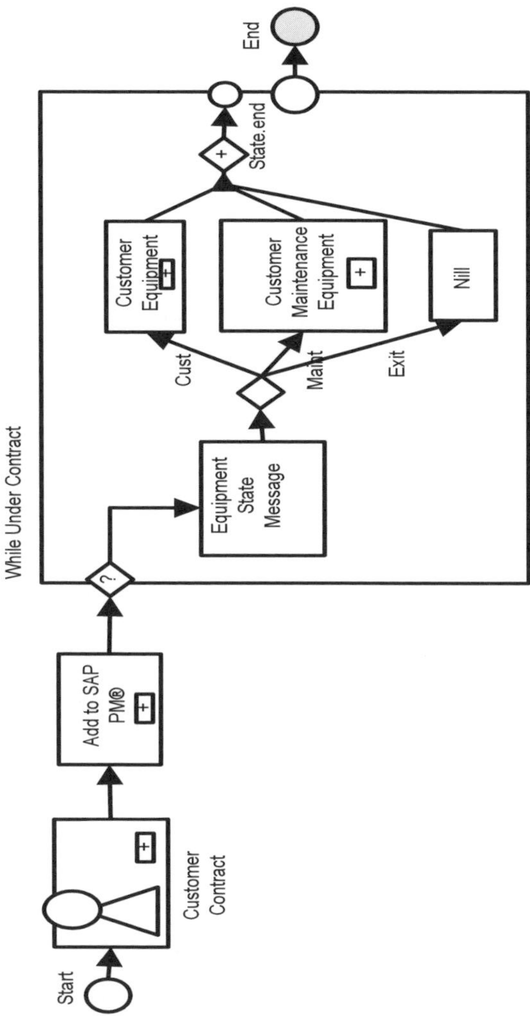

Figure 3.6 This business process diagram depicts how the Sumter Rents Maintenance Service uses the common equipment maintenance process which broadcasts a message to this process.

The business process also offers important services for the maintenance customers who want a history of work that has been done on the equipment. This maintenance history increases the value of Sumter's capital investment because it increases the resale value of the equipment.

Sumter Rents' executives knew there was profit in offering equipment maintenance to their customers, and the efficiency of the SAP PM system impressed their customers. However, to do it efficiently, the new business process would need to give customers the same service as the retail outlets. By unifying business strategy with technology, the BPM in Figure 3.6 creates new product offerings and opportunities for outsourcing.

Business Rules Subject Areas in Equipment

Because SAP handles decisions about equipment areas, there are surprisingly few business rules in the equipment process. The business process for equipment needs to manage the following decisions:

- When the schedule calls for maintenance of equipment that is assigned to customers, Sumter needs to decide when the customer should return the equipment for service. This might apply to customers who have leased the equipment for longer periods of time.
- When the manufacturer recalls equipment for safety defects, the process must decide when the recall warrants retrieval from the customer.
- When the customer returns equipment, the process should validate the data on the check-in form. Much of the maintenance is based on odometer hours. Since it is easy for the equipment technician to make an error in entering the usage hours, business rules should look and verify this data.
- The business process needs a business rule to map the equipment attributes to the SAP PM iDoc attributes.

The process design team may begin the Business Rules Approach for these topics or detail them later. If there is a separate team developing the business rules, then they model the business rules with activity placeholders on the BPD. Figure 3.4 shows one of these business rules. Their placement is consistent with my introductory remarks about the use of the rule to control flow in the business process.

To unit test the business process, the process designers put hard-coded, or dummy, business rules into the process flow.

Customer Relationship Process

Despite a solid ERP implementation, many of Sumter Rents' retail processes are manual. Store personnel assign equipment to walk-in customers using a paper form. Large commercial customers want a more modern process, so the business process team works with the marketing team to develop the customer ordering process.

The marketing team wants to use a combination of the web model of the rental car industry, and the shopping cart of popular retail web pages. These two popular features serve as a model for the new customer relationship process. Customers will be able to choose the equipment types that they wish to rent, and select the dates they wish to lease them. If the units are unavailable on the desired dates, the system will ask them if they wish to receive an email when the equipment is available. The customer may also choose to have Sumter Rents deliver the equipment to his location.

The customer business process is presented in Figure 3.7. The process reserves available equipment for the rental period and places the selected equipment in their shopping cart. The folio prices the equipment and mobilization charges, taking into account special discounts to preferred customers using the customer discount rule. When the customer has completed his folio, he reserves the folio. The reservation is secured with a credit card, or if he is a preferred customer, he needs no further data.

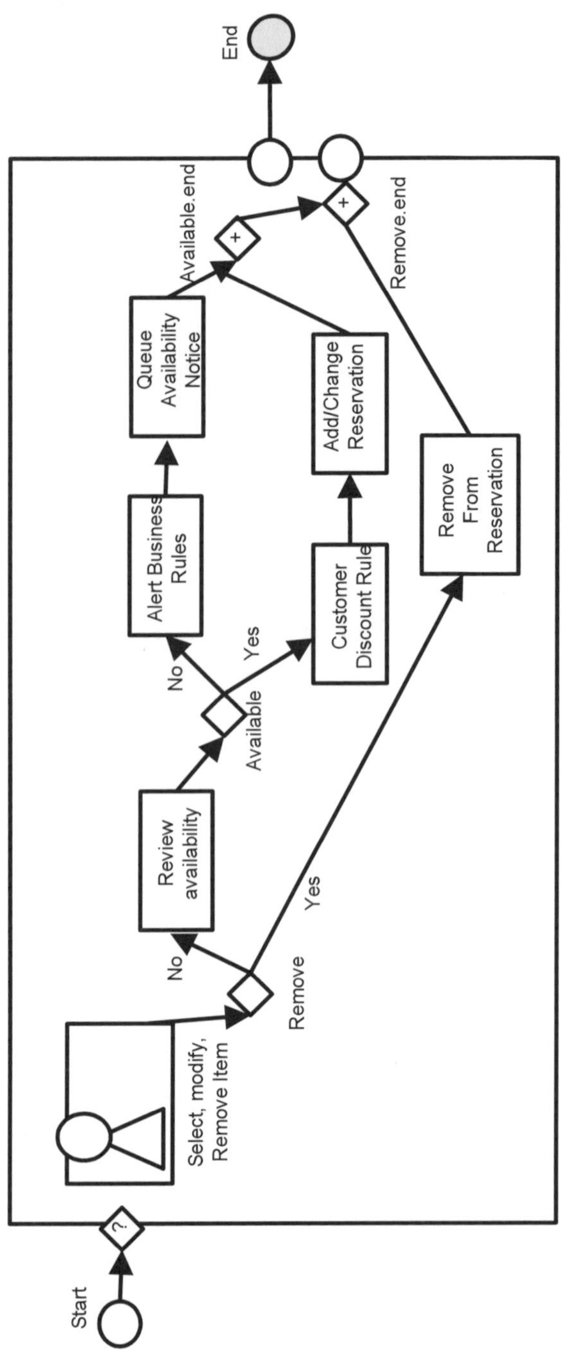

Figure 3.7 This business process diagram depicts the Sumter Rents customer folio system.

Figure 3.7 presents another example of a long-running transaction. This diagram shows how the BPM method cuts programming. In a database centric model, the state of the process would be stored in transactions. For instance, a developer might hold the details of a reservation in a table with status flags. The business process software keeps the list of equipment, thereby cutting the programming associated with user interfaces.

I have not presented all the processes needed for the customer service application. Sumter Rents aims to develop a preferred customer program to build loyalty with its largest customers. So, it will need a process for identifying such customers, and another for accepting applications. The Business Intelligence chapter will describe the method for defining which customers are candidates for preferred status.

A better business process should improve customer loyalty. Construction firms prepare quotations for competitive bids and job estimates. A bid is won or lost on a small margin, so each bid needs to contain accurate costs. In the business architecture phase, the management team suggested publishing a spreadsheet with a .NET web service component as a customer rental process. The spreadsheet allows the customer to link real-time rental costs to their bids when preparing budgets.

The customer process allows them to build a *non-singular* folio of requested equipment which remains open as long as the customer has equipment out on lease. This is another long running transaction. The customer service process adds and removes equipment to the job folio so that costs are separated according to jobs. Sumter bills the customer monthly for the equipment, according to the charges within the folio.

Customer Entities

The data concept diagram for the customer process is shown on Figure 3.8. The concept depicts the data design that occurs during the BPM design process.

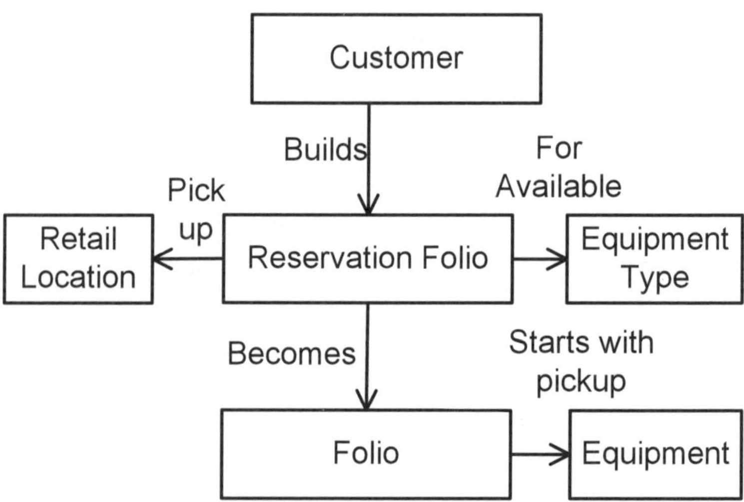

Figure 3.8 The customer process uses the customer-folio entities to manage large commercial orders for the rental of equipment.

The customer form contains the data needed to build a reservation. Preferred customers have a negotiated discount that applies to the total value of the reservation. After a reservation is made, customers are assigned the equipment of the type specified in the reservations folio.

Relations With the Equipment Process

There is an important relationship between the customer process and the equipment process. Earlier, we described a subprocess that assigns equipment to customers. The customer process tells the equipment process what equipment the store has assigned to the customer. This message style of interface allows the two processes to exist independently. This independence allows the business to make changes to the flow of the processes.

Customer service is a part of the equipment process and the customer process. There are conditions that compel servicing of equipment while the customer has it. For instance, Sumter Rents would want to bring back equipment that is out on lease if it has been the subject of a safety recall. Sumter also needs to perform critical maintenance on equipment that is on longer leases.

It is important for processes to be *loosely bound* and able to post events that communicate with other processes. Separating the processes positions them for change. A BPM suite should be able to change the processes while completing the ones that are in existence.

Business Rules Subject Areas in Customer Service

Sumter Rents aims to influence customer behavior by creating a responsive service process. These rules control the process:

- A business rule will get a customer's preferred status and apply the greatest appropriate discount to the reservation
- A business rule will decide if the customer has requested an email notice or a phone notice if the needed equipment is at a nearby retail location
- A business rule will map entries from the business process attribute into the SAP accounts payable iDOC.
- A business rule will find out if auxiliary equipment is needed based on all the equipment in the folio. The process application will suggest that they order the equipment.

The activities for two of these rules are shown on the Customer Process as Alert Business Rule and Customer Discount Rule.

Summary of Our Business Process Modeling Activities

During business process design, the earlier rapid markups we built (if any) in the architecture phase become more complex. As we develop more details, we add more of the flow control symbols to the diagram. These symbols represent the flow, steps and conditions of the business. For instance, in the interview we discovered that different schedules and events cause maintenance on the equipment. BPML depicts a schedule as a small clock. The schedule looks in SAP PM to see if there is any maintenance, and, if so, sends a message to the equipment process which treats the message as a multiple event queue. The message decides the suitable process path.

BPML produces the BPEL that the engine uses to perform the process. BPML/BPEL coordinates activities and events in a new and effective way. In the equipment example, we needed a message-driven event that wakes up every day, or hour, to look for scheduled equipment maintenance events. With each new equipment state, a subprocess queries SAP PM for the maintenance events. From that point forward, the event message communicates the maintenance schedule to the equipment process. This is all self-contained within the long running equipment transaction. In the old way of programming, creating a message-event activity required advanced programming techniques. COTS products, such as SAP PM, manage equipment maintenance regimes well, but getting the information events to the field is complex without BPML.

Developing the Core Business Process (CBP)

Every enterprise runs its business models through a series of core business processes. I have described how some of Sumter Rents business processes support the core business architecture. These include the equipment process and the customer process. Other obvious processes are in the areas of accounting and human resources. These are the core processes that define their business.

A core business process is different from a traditional data or system process. In the past, we would create a program to send a database transaction in a flat-file to an ERP. Much of the development was about the mysterious needs of the target system and the details of the process were buried in the details of the integration. The program code did the mappings of the source attributes. The core business process is all about what the business does, irrespective of these details.

Core processes are independent of the systems that fulfill them. A traditional system is built to process specific procedures within a system; and these procedures process data and create transactions and reports. A CBP performs a goal or an activity within the business architecture. The CBP uses the application as a service that moves transactions or queues a procedure within a system.

There is another important difference: the CBP does its work through process data. The benefit of this is that managers and process administrators work with the specific instances of a process, a customer's order or a specific contract order. In a traditional system this may be a query or a report; it is not a native feature of the environment. BPM strengthens the traditional business data with descriptive process information, especially timing information for activities.

When we want them to be more efficient and controllable, core processes change internally. Enterprises use Business Process Management to fine-tune the process and make them more efficient so even the flow controls may change. There are long-term benefits for a business that uses a core process approach. By identifying core business processes, it is easier to position a service or product for outsourcing. Often, legacy systems lock important processes in a milieu of databases and point-to-point integration. This is the problem of many legacy processes; especially in government. For instance, if transportation is not the work of a COBOL mainframe program, then you can outsource your transportation needs. A core process approach unlocks your processes and positions them for worthwhile change.

As information (think of business forms) flows through a business process, every activity, decision, scope or loop may use any of the upstream process attributes (form fields). Activities have inputs and output. As the information flows along the process, an activity may use the inputs, or the outputs to calculate, decide or transform information. Diverting the data into a separate, late-binding business rules service creates more flexibility for improving business execution.

In the future, advanced organizations will view their core processes and business rules as some of their most important assets. These core processes will need stewardship. Advanced enterprises will carefully tune the basic business processes to achieve a tactical, competitive advantage. The tuning or construction occurs during the projects identified in the business architecture phase.

The core business process approach is an important modeling technique you will need to build the service oriented architecture.

The Role of the Core Business Process

Corporate leadership measures, oversees and controls the top-level processes. The structure of core processes parallels management structures. Executives monitor the top-level processes while managers measure and control at the subprocess level.

So, a process-oriented approach with BPM simplifies business activity monitoring. This is because BPM tools store and manage the business forms attached to processes at each level. In Sumter Rents' example, we will be able to answer larger scale questions such as what is the number of bulldozers in customer assignment, in maintenance, at the store, and others. Similarly, a mortgage company oversees their loan process —how many loans are in data gathering, customer credit checks, pre- and post-settlement? How long are these processes taking?

You should involve every level of the enterprise in developing the core business process. To develop the processes for Sumter Rents, we used interviewing and research techniques to detail the CBP. Executives were involved in the project start, division managers communicated concerns, and equipment managers in the retail store told the rest of the story.

To build a CBP, we start with activities: starts, stops, data flows, and subprocesses. This depends on your style; when you develop CBP, you should get the building blocks right before you put much detail into them.

We developed a logical subprocess model to improve the equipment and customer processes. We used messaging and event techniques to create a process that is independent of the external systems processing the transaction. Imagine going from a web screen to a cell phone for ordering.

Once you define and detail the core processes, you will set up each ERP, or legacy stovepipe, as a separate service. As we climb above the CBP's, we want to break out the business units in a manner that can be outsourced or in-sourced. For instance, in the business processes in Figure 3.4, the project team has set up SAP as a subprocess call. Now, Sumter Rents might decide to outsource or replace the SAP application.

Flow Control Elements for the CBP

The semantics of our requirement suggest what BPLM should be placed on the process diagram. To build a process orchestration, you match the scenarios of the process needs with a combination of BPML models. BPML tools compose a single document for each of the processes.

It is useful to understand what BPML does and how you use it to manage your processes. BPML orchestrates services and applications by bridging with web services. In the past, systems did this orchestration with hardwired computer programs and systems utilities. BPML concentrates all of this logic for building a composite application so that your application is easy to change. Again, because your team does not have to write these programs, they will spend fewer hours coding.

Setting up Business Rules Within the Business Processes

BPML often uses web services to call subprocesses, business rules and interfaces to external systems. BPML creates business process execution language (BPEL). Before we look at some BPML/BPEL, it is important to understand the Web Services Description Language (WSDL). As I mentioned in the introductory chapter, web services create the late bindings for business rules services. Common characteristics of web services are:

- Self-contained, self-describing, modular applications that are published, found, and invoked across the web.

- Software modules that "describe a collection of operations that are network-accessible through standardized XML messaging"
- Loosely coupled software components that interact with one another dynamically through standard Internet technologies.

This means that there is no other code in the business process other than the data structure that is needed to invoke the web service.

An XML WSDL specifies the web service. The major parts of the WSDL are:

- Types: data that defines the data types used in messages
- Messages: defines the data parts of a communication
- Port Types: defines the exposed operations (similar to a function call in programming languages). Usually there is an input, an output and a default port type.
- Bindings: defines the communication protocols
- Ports: specifies a port address on the web server for a binding
- Services: collects related ports.

Because the web service needs to pass information into a type or data structure, there is some inherent dependency. If you need to change the record attributes of a business rule, you will need to change the business process.

In the next chapter I will describe how a web service executes a business rule.

Business Process Modeling and BPML

Here are some of the basic BPML choices and the BPEL that supports it. You can get a comprehensive specification for BPML-BPEL at *www.bpmi.org*. A comprehensive list of BPEL tags is beyond the scope of this book. What I hope to show here is the relationship between the modeling choices, the modeling symbol and the BPEL that it creates.

Choice/Switch This is a conditional switch among several choices depending on the process path. The effect of choice and switch are similar. The Choice tag equals an *If ... Then ... Else* predicate in procedural languages. The Switch Tag equals *Case* or *switch* instructions.

In the business modeling language, these tags are shown as a series of paths and activities between the (◇) and the (⊕). The switch evaluates the conditions and selects the activity path associated with the event. For example, BPEL for the first choice in the equipment process is:

```
<switch name="Inspection"
 <case condition="Accept"
  <sequence>
  <invoke name="Add to SAP"
   partner = '...'
   inputContainer = equipmentEntity
   outputContainer=equipmentEntity
  </invoke>
  </sequence>
 </case>
<otherwise>
  <sequence>
  <invoke name="Return to MFR"
   partner = '...'
  </invoke>
   <terminate name="Terminate"
   </terminate>
  </sequence>
</otherwise>
</switch>
```

This choice is from the left side of Figure 3.3. In the BPML, the *switch* tag tells the process engine to evaluate if the equipment has passed the inspection. The name tag in BPEL is the text that is associated with the diagram.

The sequence tag defines a series of activities to do. If the program runs an activity as a web service or as a separate program, then BPEL specifies this with the invoke tag. The partner is a reference to the program or web service that is used to process the information. The input and output containers are arguments for the program or web service. The partners and containers are defined at the beginning of the BPML document.

The terminate tag is shown as a (⊗) on the process diagram.

While: The while activity executes an activity path based on the truth value of a condition. There is an example of a while loop in Figure 3.3. The equipment process uses a while activity to move equipment from the retail store to the customer and to maintenance. Within the process is an activity that waits for a message queue for the equipment. For each message there is a case that moves the equipment among the retail store, maintenance, or the customer. The idealized BPEL for this is

while name="While Inventory"

```
<sequence>
<invoke name="EquipmentState"
 partner="MessagingDestination"
 portType="MessageQueue"
 operation="receiveWait"
 inputContainer="receiveWait.Input"
 outputContainer="receiveWait.Output"
</invoke>
<switch Name ="Decision"
 <case receiveWait.Output.text="SOLD">
  <sequence>
   <empty name="Empty"
  </sequence>
 </case>
 <case receiveWait.Output.text ="RetailStore">
  <sequence>
  <invoke name="CheckIntoStore"
... -- These ellipsis denote the sub process WSDL's
  </invoke>
 </sequence>
 </case>
<case receiveWait.Output.text ="AssignCustomer">
<sequence>
 <invoke name="Lease2Customer"
... WSDL
 </invoke>
</sequence>
</case>
<case receiveWait.Output.text ="Maintenance">
<sequence>
<invoke name="CheckMain"
... WSDL
</invoke>
</sequence>
</case>
</switch>
</sequence>
</while>
```

There is a case within the while loop that moves the equipment between the customer, the retail store and maintenance.

As well as the case and while tags, there are many other important BPML constructions including:

- **Spawn** The spawn tag signals the BPEL engine to run the activities in the branches in parallel. For instance, if process A and process B can be run in parallel, then the BPML would be:

```
<sequence>
<spawn name="process A"
 partner = '...'
 inputContainer = processAEntity
 outputContainer=processAEntity>
<spawn name="process B"
 partner = '...'
 inputContainer = processBEntity
 outputContainer=processBEntity>
</sequence>
```

- **Exceptions** Business processes raise exceptions with the exception tag. BPML denotes exceptions with a (Ⓝ). The throw tag raises the exception. If a switch detects an abnormal condition then it executes a sequence of activities to recover gracefully from the exception. In this example, BPEL sets up a fault handler, "invalidData", at the top of the document:

```
<faultHandlers >
 <catch faultName="tns:invalidData"
 <sequence>
  <invoke name="Cleanup"
 </sequence>
 </catch>
</faultHandlers>
```

In the body of the BPEL, a case block may throw the exception with the throw tag:

```
<case sbynpx:lineLabel=”Case 1”>
<sequence>
<throw name=”Throw”
faultName=”tns:invalidData”
</throw>
</sequence>
</case>
```

- **Schedules/Waits** Business processes use the schedule tag ahead of a sequence of activities. The attributes of the schedule are controllable by the business process. BPML denotes schedules with a (🕐).

The point of this exercise is to show that BPEL gives you a lot of process control in an XML document. The BPEL engine uses the XML file to configure the process. Modeling notation simplifies changes to the BPML specification. In addition, BPML is straight-forward enough for non-technical people to use. So, in theory, non-technical personnel specify much of the process.

Typical Patterns for Business Rules in Processes

Because rules are changed with business rules software, a rule positioned for change makes the entire system more powerful. Managers might tighten a policy. Information managers might reduce the requirements for data. Service manager rules address a customer's special needs. Figure 3.9 shows a typical pattern for a business rules web service.

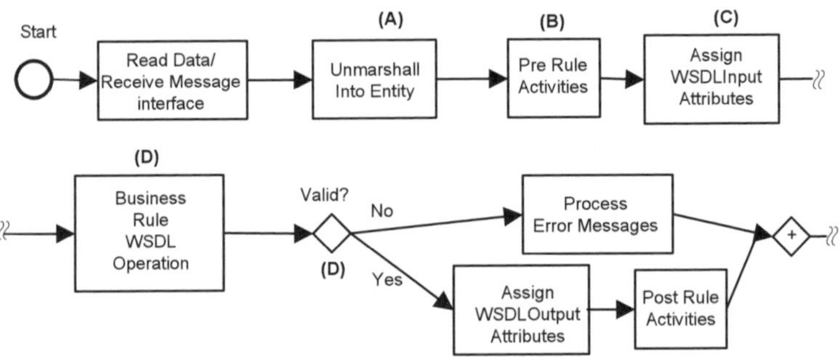

Figure 3.9 This is a typical pattern for a confirmation business rule in a business process.

Again, the figure shows a single part of a business process broken into two parts. The (≀) symbol stands for a continuation of the process from the top, upper right-hand side. If you are not familiar with business processes, the flows contain the attributes of the entities that we have described. The steps of the process are as follows:

- At the start, the process unmarshals data into the interface entity (A).
- Intervening activities may take place with the data (B).
- Activities in the process map and assign input/output attributes for the WSDL operation (C).
- The process runs the activity that invokes the web service. It uses an operation the designer has selected from the WSDL (D).

If the WSDL interface status = error *E*, then we process the error for the business rule, otherwise we continue along the other path. (This assumes the business rule directly returns error messages.)

BR's assign data to the object entity, and a CRM business rule returns a list of customer needed, or preferred, objects. A contract order rule looks at the contract number and date to lookup terms and conditions of the contract.

Interfaces for the Systems Involved

After they have detailed the core business processes, the project team should design the interfaces. They are always mindful of the needs of users. The application should not require users to enter interface data that does not reflect a business need. So, system designers should hide, or abstract, these details away from the users to the greatest extent possible. Remember that the BPM/BR should link your current networks, business systems, and applications together into a single, seamless information system—the *composite application.*

During the business process modeling phase, we developed the business's needs for a core business process. Independent of this process are the properties which the services must control in order to interface with different systems including transportation, engineering, supply chain and accounting systems.

Once there is a clear understanding of the interface's needs, then the design team maps business forms or entity data to the needs of the external systems. This suggests that they should develop a series of process activities which map the attributes of the business forms to the interfaces for the systems.

Accounting Codes In the Sumter Rents example, we have created models of the customer and the equipment processes. The models suggest different integration scenarios the production system must support. What is missing is a way to convert this data into data that the SAP accounting system uses. The design team should create maps that assign the proper transaction codes to each of these transactions.

Other Codes Applications such as SAP or Oracle Financials use specific metadata setups to your organization's data. For instance, you might have several designators for order numbers or responsible organizations. The ERP will populate columns in the database which have been labeled as placeholders. When the business process runs the interface, this information will be useful to the users of the ERP.

There are tools for developing these mappings such as SAP's *Integration Builder*. Integration Builder stores interface descriptions in a repository so that the business process can reference them. The Integration Builder publishes the interface as a web service.

It is my experience that integration teams often need to do work inward, from both sides. New and improved processes change the way an ERP is set up, and the abilities of the ERP will affect the interface processes.

Steps for Interface Success

The Sumter Design Team uses a 4 step strategy to develop the system interfaces:

1. Develop test cases for each of the scenarios for equipment maintenance and customer billing. For instance, for a selection of equipment: post a recall, test a seasonal recall, and test usage hour maintenance. The design team first tests the scenarios using SAP PM screens and reports.
2. Use SAP Interface Builder to create a web service. Create a simple business process to read a file, and then post the scenarios into the web service.
3. Add messaging to another business process. Convert the contents of the message to the data in the first scenario. Review the details of the mapping before a full integration. The design team may elect to use the Business Rules Approach to perform some of the mapping.
4. Complete the integration. The team does not try to move data all the way through until they have both sides working

It may not be possible to test every case; for example, there is a wide range of maintenance schedules. The steps above were designed to corroborate that interface processes work, assuring that the data gets to the process, before they are added to the core process.

In summary: you will want to test your examples in the test instance using a simple interface. It is easier to work with a flat file of the scenarios, loading them into the interface subprocesses, before you do this with a more involved messaging strategy.

Working with an ERP interface can be tedious and difficult. Without some experience in your team, it is risky to try this work. However, the software industry is simplifying the chore of building interfaces. BPML suites provide standard interfaces for many ERP systems. These are known as adapters. Adapters reduce the time, cost, complexity, and skills needed to integrate the core business process. The software industry offers a comprehensive set of adapters, and they work seamlessly with many BPM environments.

Connecting to External Partners

When you connect your organization to external partners, your team will use open business-to-business (B2B) protocols such as EDI and B2B business protocols. They will also need to consider *enveloping protocols* which involve exchanging transactions in a secure way and assuring that the intended recipient is the actual recipient. BPM tools support existing standard protocols, with pre-built business protocol pipelines. They also provide the tools and framework to create and adopt new protocols and to build custom pipelines.

A BPM suite will provide validation, logging, and reporting powers so that you add process steps and business rules, tailoring them to address the particular needs of each eBusiness challenge.

Trading partners might exchange information with Collaboration Protocol Agreements (CPAs), which are described at www.ebxml.org. Otherwise you may want to build trading partner profiles manually. Each trading partner profile should be identified by a unique ID determined by the enterprise. Delivery channels for acknowledgments, compression, industry-standard encryption and decryption, and non-repudiation should be configured.

At run time, the business process tracks all steps, from the first receipt of the message, to final delivery to the trading partner. You will need tools for recovering and filtering tracked message and envelope information.

The Complete Business Process Model

To complete a business process, the team details the diagram with the necessary scheduling, exceptions and structures of the messages. The purpose of the details is to erect a more complete process model. The business processes should act on all the messages, including the system failures. In the real world, business processes are more complex than the first draft:

- The process should handle every possible exception, there are two types of these: business rules exceptions and system exceptions
- The process should *compensate* for transactions that fail to complete. In a compensation, the process cleans up or backs out records from ERPs
- Prerequisite processes must complete, and there could be *delay* actions noted on the diagram.

Business processes usually receive a message and translate that message into yet another message which is understood by the next part of the process. Depending on the BPM tool that you are using, the team will need to add implementation code to the diagram for this purpose.

You can model BP's with advanced abilities that suspend processing, or communicate with disconnected, mobile processes. These powers yield opportunities for the enterprise to fine-tune their most complicated practices. They are also positioned to add new technology such as RFID.

Timing is a new type of input into Business Intelligence analysis. An analysis of this data provides places where the business can improve its processes. One improvement might be the removal of unnecessary roadblocks by rewriting hardwired processes and creating even looser coupling for flexibility.

Scheduling

BPM suites should provide integrated scheduling and control solutions for all business processes. Most suites have a process control tool that centralizes all procedural business and data processing needs into a simple, consistent, easy-to-administer application. It should support processes in a way that non-technical personnel control them.

The business process should be as automatic as possible. There are still many reasons that change schedules. Personnel work during limited hours. Critical data might be posted at a date and time that changes. The manager and business administrators understand the schedules and flow of the business better than the systems administrator or database administrator. Often, these schedules are fluid and changing, and the BPM environment should reduce your dependency upon technical personnel. A schedule editor should be available for the design group to use daily. The manager is freed from going through technical layers to control his or her systems.

Compensations and Exceptions

Certification that all sequences of activities actually complete and are orderly is a key aim of aggregating business processes and web services. Since transactions in a business process approach might require long periods of time to run through to completion, traditional mechanisms for doing this are not always applicable. Your processes must continue to run despite unpredictable circumstances. The idea of the long running transaction relies on groupings of smaller transactions. Therefore, your process will need to be able to undo the effects of a process that fails to complete.

The process design team should design the fault handlers to deal with exceptions during normal processing. They design compensation handlers which reverse the effect of a finished unit of work in a business process. The process invokes the compensation when the normal work of the process is finished. This cleans up the process for the compensation handler to start its reversal activity. The business process starts the compensation handlers by the fault handler of an enclosing scope. The block of activities decides which compensations to process. Also, it decides what order to roll back partial work if there is failure.

A modern business process environment should report to systems administrators when exceptional processes exceptions occur. The process should be able to recover and restart. Systems monitors should be able to view errors and restore the process to its original state. I will discuss exception handling in greater detail in the systems administration chapter of this book.

Testing the Business Process Model

Even if the project team needs to work on business rules, they should unit test the processes that they have developed. Testing helps detect and diagnose performance problems before the team finishes the entire project. If there are incomplete business rules, the project members might hand-code sample business rules into dummy subprocesses.

If the team spends time testing these early prototypes, they will create the final product more thoroughly and in less time. They will also be able to catch more defects, and release better projects. The other benefit to this early testing is that non-technical business analysts quickly build and document test cases. This will cut testing time. Furthermore, test documentation and test automation get combined into one formal effort.

Process performance is always a big concern of all the participants in the project. In the Sumter Rents example, there will be thousands of equipment processes running on the server. The Sumter Rents enterprise experiences various business peaks. Testing and tuning for this peak mitigates the risk of poor performance. And like the value of knowing your daily load, understanding your business peaks allows you that much more leverage when it comes time to perform a major functional upgrade or technology refresh.

Because business activities or functional areas have historical information, the data needed for business peaks should be easy to identify. A key to stress testing is to ensure that the team has enough data to do the job of stress testing.

SUMMARY

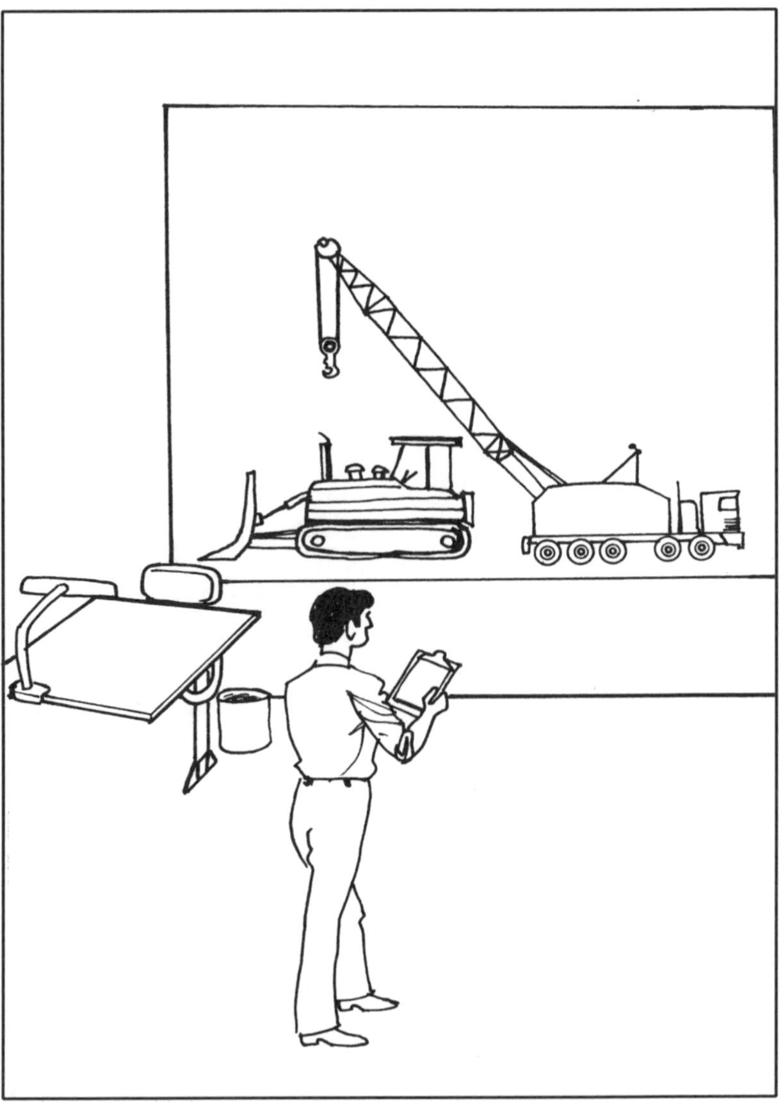

Sumter's equipment processes should improve the productivity of the team..

Successful companies, such as Sumter Rents, organize and run their business activities in an efficient way. These companies fulfill their core activities on time and with constrained budgets and personnel. But to stay competitive in today's markets, successful companies must adjust their business activities to the marketplace. They need to have these activities complete quickly with higher quality and lower costs. Because companies aim to improve their processes, they are exploring the benefits and potential competitive advantages of Business Process Management (BPM) systems. BPM offers improved efficiencies because they improve the scheduling, execution and overseeing of business activities.

Business Process Modeling enables *late binding* software architecture. This new technology can enable higher independence among the processes, which is the purpose of service oriented architectures (SOA). So, if you build a business process with BPML, it is should be easier to change business processes and the systems that support them. An activity might provide an interface to an application on a server in the technical infrastructure, yet any system that can provide the service could replace it. With a low dependency on the service (that is, the legacy system) the core business process manages the content and timing of the information sent to those systems which provide services.

There are many benefits in using a BPML approach to the SSO. By breaking a business into a series of discrete, core processes, a company might either offer that service to customers or outsource the service to others.

At some point, the business process should deal with the documents that become the transactions in the system. This is where controlling the business process with business rules becomes important. For example, a purchase order or requisition against a contract might need multiple confirmations before the system accepts it. Is the item requisitioned part of the contract? Are there delivery quantities left? Is this the best contract vehicle for the requisition? The approach that I am describing here suggests that these design questions be captured as an activity in the business process and then detailed in the business rules phase.

Because they control process flow, business rules also create business events. This is the way an evaluation of a business rule sets business processes in motion. Typical events may include reviews, approvals, product inspections, laboratory tests, maintenance inspections, and financial penalties.

Here are the bullet points of this chapter:

- In the BPM, the design team develops the core business process from interviews and research.
- Core business processes perform independently of the systems that provide services to them. The core process should also be reasonably independent of the data entry methods.
- All business processes contain flow control elements that orchestrate the process.
- Business rules set the parameters that affect flow-control in the business process.
- As well as enforcing stated policies, you discover powerful control of business processes by examining the flow of the process. Deciding when to take a path within a business process is a good place for a business rule.
- Business process modeling (BPM) notation produces BPEL. BPEL is a standard that is utilized by any BPEL engine.
- BPML has a simple and powerful syntax.
- Interfaces should be designed after the core business process is designed.
- The complete business process handles exceptions and allows transaction to be rolled back with compensations.

CHAPTER FOUR

Business Rules

Business rules decide using current information and guidelines. Organizations might change their guidelines, yet rarely will they change the subject of the rule or policy. Predictably, Sumter Rents will always have policies on customer credit, equipment maintenance and working inventory. What will change are the specifics of the rules: the discount ranges and whom they award them to, or the flexibility of changes in maintenance schedules.

Business rules software manages the rules. For instance, with business rules, Sumter Rents creates discount incentives on equipment in an off-season by updating data in the software. The Business Rules Approach develops these rules to incorporate new conditions, lessons learned, and other changes which are then introduced through the software.

As I mentioned earlier, you should isolate your corporate business rules according to core business processes needs. Interfaces and adapters use information processing rules to map process data. The business process work that we have done for the Sumter Rents projects has identified decision areas for maintenance and customer ordering and information processing rules for SAP. Classic business rules examples could be a credit worthy customer or an active contract. These areas should control or constrain business activities across the organization.

The rules team will develop business rules which follow what I call the four C's: Classify Calculate, Compare and Control. Each step of the Business Rules Approach develops these.

To discover business rules, you should start by building a library of the basic terms of the business. After you develop the basic terms, you then discover special types of these terms from the goals of the business rule. With this library of business terms, your efforts have positioned you to create rules that control business decision areas. You manage this information in a business rules repository. In this chapter, we will develop some business rules for the decision areas in Sumter Rents.

Sumter's process design team has developed solid prototypes to support the equipment maintenance and customer service projects. As a next step to support the project objectives, the business rules team analyzes the information and conducts interviews to discover the business rules. They develop the policies and constraints of these rules by reviewing documentation, caucusing managers and holding workshops.

As in Business Process Management, the rules team develops rules with a cross functional team. Because Sumter headquarters sets equipment policies, and the retail store carries them out, the business rules team canvasses a wide range of viewpoints. Basing an understanding of the current policies through individual, isolated interviews is unwise. The rules team has found that these teams are able to expose the real rules, and produce great insight and reality into the policies.

Divining the line between management and technical terms is not an easy task because not all business terms are non-technical. Business managers often speak in jargon that is either technical or nearly technical out of a necessity to discuss large business processes in meaningful shorthand. Business rules must be able to use these terms to dissect the policies, objectives and constraints into technical specifications.

In a Business Rules Approach, the team learns the semantics of a language for specification. The language connects terms and ideas to technical data in the business rules repository. The project team will need to perform technical steps. However, business members specify the key parts of the ideas.

The team confirms the rules with an analytical process that is provided by the business rules tools. This analysis should identify incongruence in the logic of the rules such as unresolved paths, redundant values assigned across the same rule set and unresolved terms.

The analysts develop the business rules through a process of defining terms; then by connecting records, computations and constraints to these terms. They do this with an understanding of the controls which the process will need.

Using a formal statement, rules are entered into the business rules repository. Next, the repository exposes the rules as a web service. The business rules team is also responsible for analyzing rule sets for consistency and completeness.

So there are two groups of steps in this activity: gaining the understanding needed to create the business rules, and the act of creating the business rules. In this section I am going to focus on what the analyst does to understand the business rule.

SUMTER BUSINESS RULES

During the Business Process Management activity, the team identified places in the flow that would benefit from a Business Rules Approach. In all, the process team identified 3 decision areas that need business rules analysis. These are:

1. Policies for retrieving equipment from customers when maintenance is called for.
2. Rules for validating the equipment inspection data before they are sent to SAP PM.
3. Assigning the proper discount to a customer's order.

In addition to these business activities, there are data processing areas that benefit from the Business Rules Approach; such as converting customer order process data into SAP iDOC.

Moreover, Sumter Rents wants to target its most profitable customers for loyalty programs. To do this, the company needs to know more about its customers. It needs to broadcast this information to the company's marketers and customer service representatives.

Policies, Constraints (Offering and Negotiations)

Most experts consider business rules to be a formal way of connecting the enterprise's policies and constraints to the information systems. A policy is a plan, or course of action, that is intended to influence and cause decisions, actions, and other matters. So, policies are designed to insure that organizations operate with guidelines in a healthful, nurturing and safe way. A constraint restricts, limits, or regulates; a check. So, operating in constraints prevents errors and mistakes. The rules we have identified for Sumter Rents information systems are examples of corporate policies and constraints. Sumter insures their investment in equipment with their automated equipment maintenance policies. Sumter also aims to raise customer loyalty through their policies. Thus, business rules formalize critical information processing aspects of an enterprise's business model.

An offering is a type of policy which is interesting to the marketing team. Part of Customer Relationship Management (CRM) develops sales campaigns, or offerings, which raise a business's *wallet share* of a customer. A campaign may be a temporary circumstance targeted to a particular customer: During a business process, a business rule could suggest products that might appeal to that customer. So, CRM models are well served by the business rule concept.

A negotiation is another type of policy that is designed to secure the best value for purchases from trading partners. The organization develops business rules for getting the best price for a purchase from a business process. They might use business rules to make offers and counter offers.

Business rules help organizations comply with government regulations. Environmental agencies limit pollution that is emitted in the air and water. When these values are exceeded, the enterprise must produce timely reports. This is another area where a business might benefit from a Business Rules Approach.

Obviously, business rules are intimately involved in the way organizations conduct business, and finance their operations. Business rules protect assets by guarding the way they are managed.

The Four C's

If policy is similar to a computer program, then a business rule is a block of code or a procedure that supports the policy. A business rule is a pro forma specification of a part of a policy or constraint's requirement. The action of the business rule is to define what a business does with the data.

Every business rule does what I call the four C's. Each business rule should classify, calculate, compare and control. They:

- **Classify** the type, the division, the sort. Sumter has at least two types of customers: the preferred customer and the ordinary customer. Sumter has many different maintenance types—seasonal maintenance, winterizing, periodic, lubricate every 400 hours and manufacturer recall. A concise business rule will start by filtering what it is deciding upon.
- **Calculate**, compute formulas, look up data and statistics, and transform and assign values. Constraints are often numerical: How long has the customer leased the equipment? How much of the credit have we extended to the customer? I have included queries and transformations in the computations. A transformation rule converts input values into useful data.
- **Compare** the calculation to the redline. The redline is a key value that must be reached, or not exceeded, or within a specified range.

- **Control** what is true or valid, correct or mistaken, and the messages that go with them. Policies are often qualitative: companies reward preferred customers and good employees.

With all these parts, the Business Rules Approach develops decisions. I am going to describe how Sumter's team developed the rules needed to finish the business processes.

Of all the C's, the most critical parts of a business rule are the redlines and thresholds of the Compare. These are the turning points of the decision. If the value of a calculation is above, below or within a threshold, then the rule accepts or rejects. Sometimes the threshold is a list. Imagine a status flag that stands for a failed or broken item. There might be several of these which managers change when there is a change in policies.

The Business Rules Approach is a powerful way to control critical details of information processing. In our conversations about Sumter Rents, we will define these controls through the 4 C's.

Using the Business Rules Software

The business rules team should use software to manage business rules. Examples are Pega™, Corticon™, and iLog.™ These products allow you to enter the business rules so the rules engine unambiguously translates them into instruction steps. Most of these products can expose the rules to business processes as a web service.

The power of using this software is in the ease that businesses change their policies and constraints. Usually, the business rules software can immediately carry out changes to the processes that use them. Alternatively, business rules might have effective dates that are set.

A Process for the Business Rules Approach

In my experience, business rules change more frequently than processes. So, business rules analysis is not always a subsequent activity to business process modeling. Rules should be independent of individual processes. A project might involve improving or developing new business rules. As we described, process modeling invoke business rules when they arbitrate the message's content that is passed among flows among activities.

A business process for the Business Rules Approach is presented in Figure 4.1.

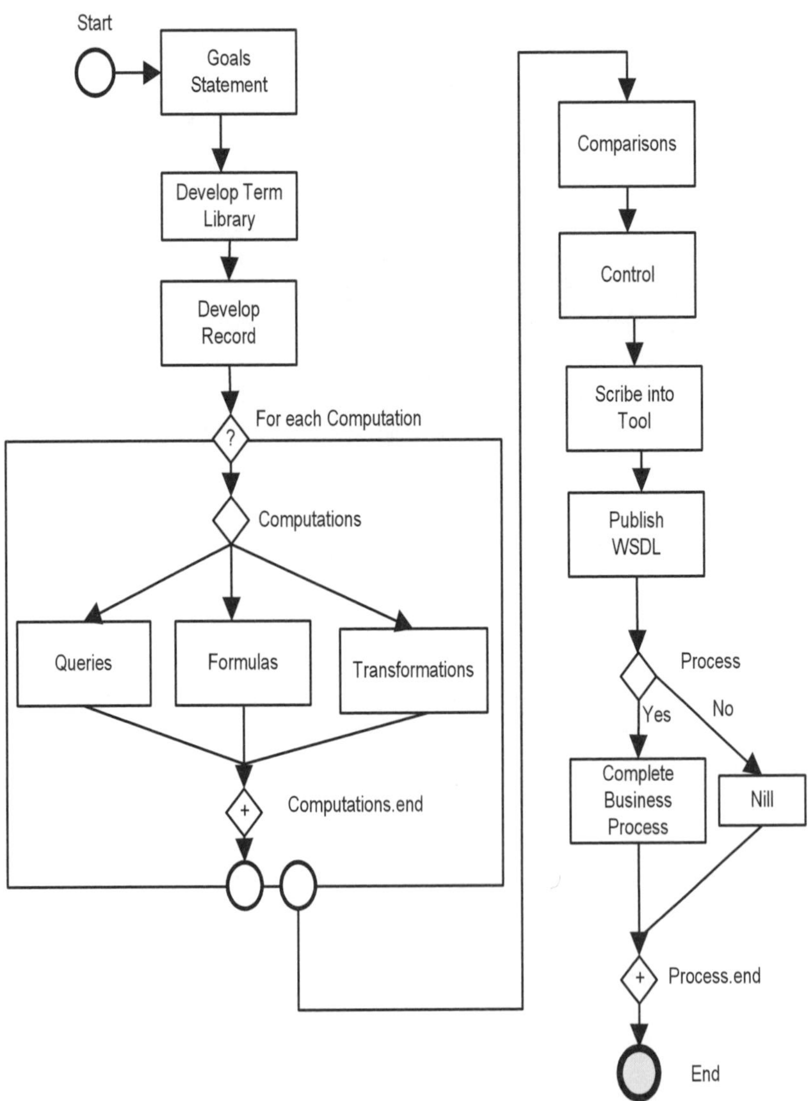

Figure 4.1 A process for developing business rules.

The process applies to each business rule in the project. The workshop's first activity is to agree upon a definitive goal statement for each of the four business rules. The goal must define the outcome of the rule, if it succeeds or fails. The language of the rule suggests the data, the computations, control and outcome.

Business Rules Activities

The business rules approach is a new design method that is understandable by the manager as well as the technologist. Business managers, executives and accountants use rules to set the policies and constraints. In a project, business rules carry out the goals that the team set up for each subject area. For instance, a goal might be to limit new product orders to the customer's credit limit. The rules must classify the customer's credit limit, calculate the new and old orders, compare the number with the credit limit, then control the ordering process. The redline in this business case is the credit limit.

Business rules use the values of the data in a business form (requisition, reservation) as a basis for each decision. The goal of the business rules suggests the needed information. Rules assign meaning to the values of a business form entry. The business rules software needs a dictionary of terms to do this, but I'll discuss that next. In the Sumter Project, the two business forms we are working with are the Customer Folio and the Equipment Maintenance Work Order. Business rules use the values from the fields in these forms. These fields are known as parameters. Figure 4.2 presents the maintenance work order form that is produced by SAP PM. The form is either printed out or emailed to the equipment manager for the store.

Sumter Rents Maintenance Work Order

Maintenance Order:MN00Z0

Equipment Id:98034

Model/Serial Number: CAT D6H

Assigned Store:Huntsville

Prn Date: 08/15/2006

Schedule date: 08/19/2006

Odometer Reading(hr):3416

Work Items:
1. 1600 Hr Lubrication, see manual: D6H, 1998, pg 134
2.
3.
4.

Work location:

Completed:

Figure 4.2 Business processes work with virtual business forms. For instance, the maintenance process works with this form.

Throughout the business rule design, the teams develop a dictionary of terms, or parameters, for each rule. These terms signal the flavors of things—a code value for a preferred customer, a delivery mode for a truck, or even numeric data such as ranges and limits.

With the dictionary of terms, the business rules team assembles data records for the business rules to use. In transformations, business rules might look up referential data to assign values to the fields. Many business rules make their decisions on values in more than one field. These records complete the information needs of the rules.

Optionally, the team might decide to develop a fact diagram or concept diagram to assess the business goals and the computations needed in processing the data records. For example, utilities, which are powered by database queries, are needed in order to bring back supplemental or referential data, or to add or count the values of events.

I consider queries and transformations of data to be a type of computation. Computations assign data to records. For instance, in the customer ordering application, the rule must return the customer's discount value to the business process. Computations might include formulas, selections of data such as the maximum or minimum value, or statistical trends.

Sometimes computations within a business rule are the basis for facts in Business Intelligence. The building blocks for a data warehouse include basic retail queries such as which items were sold, to whom were they sold, and when were they sold. Guidelines and policies might affect this information. In a Business Intelligence application, business managers review performance indicators which the data warehouse publishes using business rules.

Business rules software will state a rule as a predicate. A predicate (*if… then …*) consists of a guard and an outcome. A guard is the Boolean term after the *if.* In the next step of the Business Rules Approach, the team defines the guard of the predicate. This is what I call the comparison part of the Business Rules Approach. Examples might include: *If a customer's credit limit is greater than x* or *If the number of unacceptable items is greater than y*, etc. In the control activity, the business rules team decides what the outcome of the predicate will be; based on simple Boolean success or failure.

The business rules software publishes the rule as a web service as described by Web Services Description Language (WSDL).

The final step for the rules method is to incorporate the web service into the business process. The process team reads the web service into the business process suite. The WSDL specifies the data that interacts with the business process. The business process invokes an operation in the service. For instance, we decided that business rules where needed to verify the odometer reading on the customer check-in form. When we have published these rules, we will add them to the processes we developed in the last chapter. The process should handle the success or failure of the business rule.

Business Rules Concepts

I have depicted the concepts that are carried out in the business rule process in Figure 4.3.

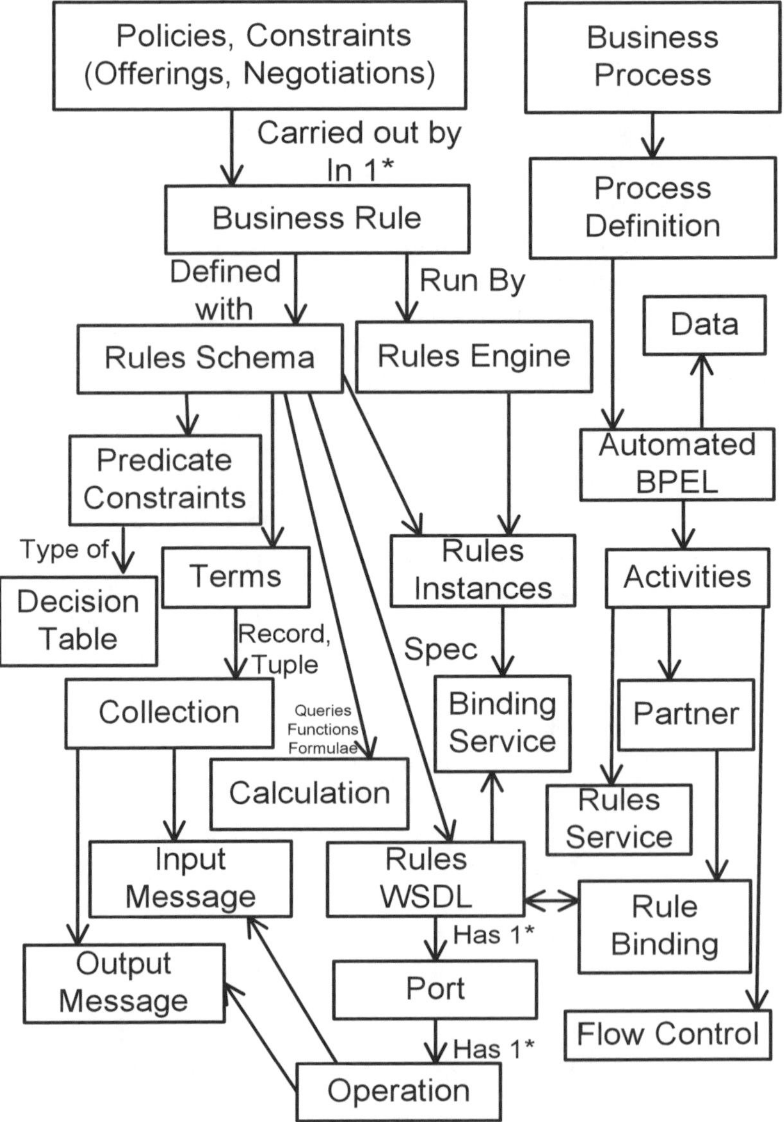

Figure 4.3 This concept schema depicts the things that compose the business rule and its relationship to the business process.

The business rule is an expression of an enterprise's policies or constraints. The Business Rules Approach allows a flexible fine-tuning of the tactics that a competitive organization needs.

My approach to business rules is to break the idea into predicate constraints, terms, and computations. Predicate constraints are the *if... then ... else* clauses of the language. Designers use the terms to create collections of data, or records. Also, the rule uses the data terms to perform calculations; including equations and queries. Business rules use each of these data structures to perform their computations.

The information in the business rules schema creates two critical elements: the metadata and the web service specification, which gets used in the business process. The diagram shows that the "Rules WSDL" web service is a virtual doorway to the business rule engine. The doorway passes information back and forth between the process and the engine via the input message and the output message created by the business rule. When the service evaluates the business rule, the engine runs the computations and subsequent steps. If the web service is like a doorway, then the binding service is the pathway for the information.

In the last chapter we described how the design team found out where to place business rules in the process. The first parts of the BPEL define the services that the partners provide. One of those partners is a business rules service. When you connect the business process with the rules service, the BPM software will need the business rules WSDL to create the service specification. Most BPML software will incorporate every port and operation in the description. The rule in the business process uses only one port. When it is time to run a business rule, the business process engine prepares an input message and sends it to an operation. The service returns an output message.

Equipment Maintenance for Sumter Rents

Sumter's equipment managers must keep the customers and their management happy.

Equipment is Sumter's largest capital investment. Proper maintenance, while a daunting task, is critical to the preservation of that investment. Scheduled maintenance might come due while a piece of equipment is out on rental. Fetching equipment from customers can be harmful to the productivity of both Sumter and the customer, so Sumter needs to put in place rigorous policies regarding how this issue is handled. If Sumter Rents must recall the equipment, then it should replace the equipment with an equivalent item. So there might be two rules variations: a rule for when to exchange the equipment and a rule for when to bring back the equipment.

Sometimes manufacturers discover safety defects in their products, and issue recall notices to customers. In this case, Sumter immediately brings back or repairs the equipment. If equivalent equipment is available, then the customer is provided with a replacement.

Most of Sumter Rents heavy equipment must undergo full lubrication every 400 to 600 hours of operation, or every 6 months. Heavily used equipment needs frequent service, and preferred customers often lease this equipment for periods that exceed this limit.

When equipment is returned from a customer, the equipment manager enters the operation hours into an equipment return form. It is easy to misenter the reading, and this might miscue the schedule in SAP PM. Until the equipment's onboard computer data are available through RFID, Sumter will need to develop a logical check for data. For instance, if the engine hours are less than preceding recorded hours, then the odometer reading is wrong.

Maintenance Goals

The business rules team holds meetings and workshops to develop the rules for the maintenance business process. The cross functional team includes the top management of equipment, a director of customer quality and equipment managers from the retail stores. They reach a consensus on the policies for maintaining the customer assigned equipment. They agree on a goal of how to decide when to bring back the equipment from the customer in case of scheduled maintenance or manufacturer recall. The rules team states the goals as follows:

- If equipment is scheduled for maintenance and the reason is not a manufacturer recall, and the customers lease is greater than a set period (Let's call the period between the scheduled maintenance and the tolerance for replacement, *replacement time tolerance.*), and there is replacement equipment available, then bring back the equipment from the customer and replace it with an equivalent piece of equipment.

- If equipment is scheduled for maintenance and the maintenance is not a manufacturer safety recall, and the customer's lease is greater than another set period (Let's call the period between the scheduled maintenance and the greatest time for delay in maintenance, *greatest time tolerance.*), and there is no replacement equipment available, then bring back the equipment from the customer, repair it and return it.
- If the equipment is scheduled for maintenance and the maintenance is a safety recall, then bring back the equipment. If equivalent equipment is available, then replace the equipment.

I suggest that every goal should be stated as a predicate (*if* … *then* … *else*). The texts *Business Rules Applied,* by Ross, or *The Business Rules Approach, by* Halibern, present many different approaches to defining business rules. However, you might also use a form that more specifically suits your needs. Your rules should be concise and non-technical. Note the three goals are separate and their execution is not dependent on order.

Usually, Sumter should have replacement equipment for the customer. Some of the equipment, however, might be rare, or in high demand, and Sumter might not have an available replacement.

We see that there are two different (time) redlines that would cause the equipment manager to bring back the equipment. The equipment maintenance subprocess in chapter 3 will continue to check these times until the equipment is returned, or until time has passed one of the threshold values. There are no fixed constants for the time that will cause the business rule to fire an action in the business process. Rather, the time varies with the urgency of the maintenance. For instance, we would not want to return a bulldozer when all that is needed is a small, non-critical task. Ideally, the business should build a decision table for the maintenance to be performed and the associated times. I have presented a decision table in Table 4.1.

Maintenance Type	*Replacement Time*	*Maximum Time*
Recurring Lubrication	30 Days	50 Days
Manufacturer Recall Minor	60 Days	90 Days
Manufacturer Recall Major-Safety	1 day	1 Day
Other	60 Days	90 Days

Table 4.1 Redline values for the type of maintenance and the allowable schedule slippage. The replacement time is the allowable period that the manager can wait for the return of the equipment when there is an equivalent replacement available for the customer's leased equipment. The maximum time is the greatest time that the manager waits regardless of available equipment.

Business rules software allows managers to change these times and add more maintenance types and times.

The details of what the business rules must perform are as follows:

- **Maintenance Event Data Elements:** The important data elements for the maintenance business rule include the date of the scheduled maintenance, the current date, the equipment identifier, the equipment maintenance types and the customer's location. These fields suggest the keys for a logical record for the maintenance business rule.
- **Maintenance Event Classification:** The rule classifies the maintenance. There is a separate goal for manufacturer recall.
- **Maintenance Event Computations:** There are three computations:
    1. The category of maintenance identifies the redline values from the maintenance type decision table.
    2. The time from the schedule to the current date sets the days from the scheduled maintenance.
    3. A data query discovers available replacement equipment.
- **Maintenance Event Comparison:** The rule compares the redline values against the number of days from the current date.
- **Maintenance Event Control:** If the time elapsed has passed the replacement time, return a message that the customer's equipment should be replaced with an equivalent unit. If the time elapsed has passed the maximum time, then return a message for personnel to at once to bring back the equipment. In these cases, the value of the business rule should be *false*, or *invalid* and error messages should be sent to the process.

Some maintenance type codes define a recurring lubrication. In configuring a business rules engine, the analysts either create a function that looks at the list to decide that it is a recurring lubrication, or they create multiple entries in the decision table. These entries would list the technical values for the maintenance type. However, this would make the decision table more technical and less accessible to managers.

The query that looks for a replacement equipment type would scan the operational data store described in the previous chapter. Customers reserve equipment by category, so data in the customer relationship process influences this business rule.

When computations are identified with a dictionary term, other business rules reuse these computations and classifications. The business rules repository should allow the analyst to name the computation with a familiar business term. The Business Rules Approach builds a library of these terms. Some Business Rules Approach Analysts consider these separate business rules.

This finishes the business rule definition for the customer issued, maintenance event business rule.

Odometer Rules

The business rules design team next turns their focus to the rules for certifying the odometer reading (miles and hours) for equipment whose maintenance schedule calls for a correct value. When the customer returns equipment to a retail store, the rental technician fills out an equipment inspection form. Since the store clerks manually read the odometer, their errors have created miscues in SAP PM. For instance, if a clerk *boxes*, or inverts two numbers then the number might be an order of magnitude smaller. An invalid entry might cause a mistaken maintenance order.

The team designs this business rule to avert a simple data error by looking at the information in the system's operational data store. They base the rules on a logical examination of the data:

- If the equipment calls for an odometer reading and the odometer reading is less than the preceding reading then reject the input value.
- If the equipment calls for an hours odometer reading and the odometer reading is greater than 80% of the hours the customer had equipment, then reject the input value.

This set of business rules decides when to accept or reject the odometer readings fed to SAP PM to trigger maintenance work orders. You see that there are no constant redline values for odometer readings.

The business rule follows theses steps:

- **Odometer Reading Data Elements:** The important data elements are the equipment identifier, a customer identifier, the equipment type and the odometer reading.
- **Odometer Reading Classification:** The rule classifies the equipment as calling for an odometer reading. The rule classifies the odometer reading type: hours or miles.
- **Odometer Computations:** There are 3 computations:
    1. The equipment type controls whether the equipment needs an odometer reading.
    2. A query recalls the preceding odometer reading.
    3. A query computes the maximum probable usage hours. Construction crews often use the equipment 20 hours a day, so this maximum time is computed as 20 times the number of days (or fraction).
- **Odometer Reading Comparison:** The input odometer reading is compared with the preceding odometer reading and the maximum probable odometer reading.
- **Odometer Reading Control:** If the odometer reading is less than the preceding odometer reading or greater than the maximum probable reading, then return a message stating the user has mistaken the odometer reading. In these cases, the value of the business rule should be *false*, or *invalid*. It might be expedient for the rule to provide the earlier odometer reading in the error message.

You might connect the odometer rules with the customer maintenance event rule. It seems that when odometer hours drive critical maintenance, there is a gap of information while the customer has the equipment. A suggested improvement would be to estimate the hours of use while a construction contractor has leased the equipment, and then anticipate when the next maintenance should be performed.

Equipment Maintenance Data Concepts

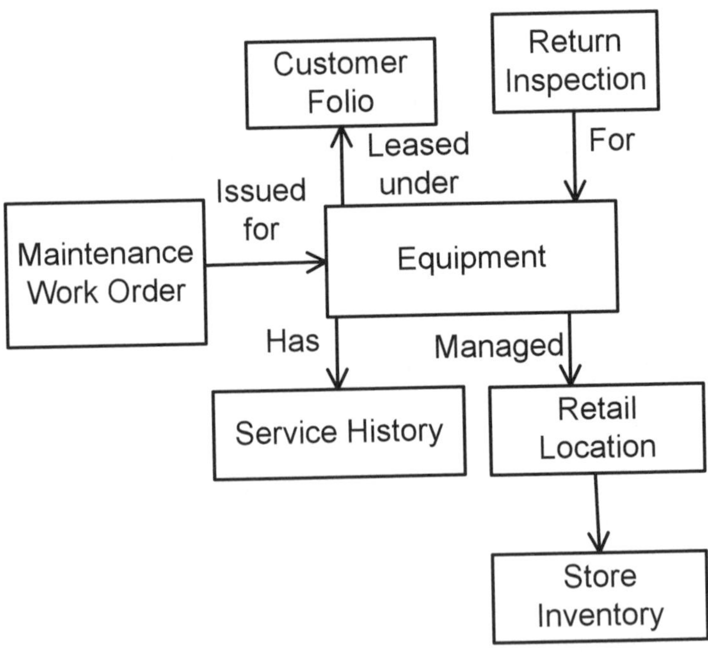

Figure 4.4 This concept schema depicts the data composition of the business rules for customer maintenance returns and the odometer reading.

The business rule presumes the queries are available for data shown in the concept diagram, Figure 4.4. In the concept, the equipment is assigned to a customer and it is the target of a current maintenance work order. The customer maintenance business rule will need to query the work order category. Next it will need to find out if there is equipment of the same classification available in the store inventory.

When the customer returns the equipment, a store clerk finishes a return inspection. The clerk enters the odometer reading as a part of the inspection. The business rule will need to query for the class of odometer (hours, mileage) reading and the preceding odometer reading.

When the business process is ready to run this business rule it should provide the needed data. The customer maintenance business rule will need a simple record type that is expressed in a data type definition:

```
<?xml version="1.0" encoding="UTF-8"?>
<!ELEMENT customerMaintenanceRule (EquipmentId,
CustomerId)>
<!ELEMENT EquipmentId (#PCDATA)>
<!ELEMENT CustomerId (#PCDATA)>
```

When the business rule is exposed as a web service, business rules software should create the data type. With the data type definition and business process software, the type is automatically incorporated into the flows.

The equipment identifier will identify its type to the business rule. The rule needs the maintenance type to find the redline value for the time. The process shown in Figure 3.4 in the preceding chapter sends a message stating that the equipment should be maintained. Queries should lookup the maintenance tickets and find the maintenance types. The location of the equipment, and the availability of the class of equipment, is developed from the customer identifier.

The odometer business rule will need a simple record type that is expressed in a data type definition:

```
<?xml version="1.0" encoding="UTF-8"?>
<!ELEMENT odometerRule (EquipmentId, OdometerReading)>
<!ELEMENT EquipmentId (#PCDATA)>
<!ELEMENT OdometerReading (#PCDATA)>
```

The equipment identifier finds the equipment type and the need for an odometer reading. Similarly, the preceding odometer reading is available from the equipment identifier.

These record types are used as input for the WSDL. Later, I will describe how the web service performs the business rule and how it interacts with the process.

Customer Business Rules

Next, the business rules team develops the rules needed for the customer relationship business process. The cross functional team includes marketing management, the manager of customer contracts and the retail store managers. The teams explore two rule sets: a customer discount and a notice system.

Sumter gives preferred customer discounts of various amounts. Sumter also carries out short-term offerings at different locations and different times. The special offerings are for classes of construction equipment. A class of equipment might be, for example, a 4 ton bulldozer or a 5 cubic yard dump truck. The rules should compute the lowest available discount for the reserved item.

Occasionally, customers might wish to be alerted when a certain equipment type is available for leasing. The rules should limit this notice to those creating a reservation folio. The notice should be removed either after the customer accepts the equipment, or at the customer's direction.

Customer Discount

The goal of the customer discount rule is as follows:

- If the customer is a preferred customer, then find his negotiated discount. If the equipment has special discounts at the location for the stated date, then find the discount. Return the greater of the two values.
- If the customer is not a preferred customer and the equipment has special discounts at the location, then find the discount. If there is a discount the return the value.

The details of what the business rules must perform are as follows:

- **Customer Discount Data Elements:** The important data elements are the customer identifier, the equipment type and equipment location.
- **Customer Discount Classification:** The rule classifies the customer as a preferred customer.
- **Customer Discount Computations:** There are 2 computations:
    1. Using the customer identifier, look up the customer's negotiated discount.
    2. Using the retail store location and the equipment type, look up a discount for the location and the equipment type.
- **Customer Discount Comparison:** Compare and return the greater of the two discounts.
- **Customer Discount Control:** The discount will be applied to the estimated bill for the customer's rental folio. The rule should always return a *true* and an assigned discount of zero or greater.

This business rule allows the store managers to create short-term rental incentives. During slow periods they may elect to apply a discount to unleased inventory. The managers will need the application to connect to the data that the business rule uses to compute the local discount.

Customer Notification

The goals of the customer notification business rules are as follows:

- If the customer is a preferred customer and the class of equipment for a rental order is not available and the customer has chosen to get notice of availability, then turn the notice on.
- If the customer has received the quantity and class of equipment that he requested, then turn the notice off.
- If the customer requests no further notice, then turn notice off.

The details of what the business rules must perform are as follows:

- **Customer Notification Data Elements:** The important data elements are the customer identifier, an acceptance attribute, the class of equipment and the order number that holds the store location of the equipment and the rental time frame.
- **Customer Notification Classification:** The rule classifies the customer as a preferred customer. The rule classifies the acceptance attribute as affirmative.
- **Customer Notification Computations:** There are 2 computations:
    1. From a query, discover if the store has issued all the items the customer has requested. This query uses the order number.
    2. From a query, find out if the class of equipment is available at the location for the rental period. This query uses the equipment identifier.
- **Customer Discount Comparison:** Check the availability of equipment in the preferred class, at the specified location for that date.
- **Customer Discount Control:** When there is available equipment, notify the customer through the manner requested.

The primary users of this notice were customers needing a short-term lease of equipment that is in high demand. To use this feature, they would create a reservation for equipment they know is not immediately available.

When other customers return equipment, and the store inspects it, they receive a notice from the retail store that it is available.

The management team considered many ideas in developing this rule. They considered adding a model to the prompting list; so the customer could be more specific about the notice. For instance, the customer may want a Caterpillar® versus a Kubota®. Because of the service oriented approach, this rule should be simple to add later.

Customer Data Concepts

As in the maintenance customer rules, there must be queries that support the needed calculations. Figure 4.5 shows the concepts for this.

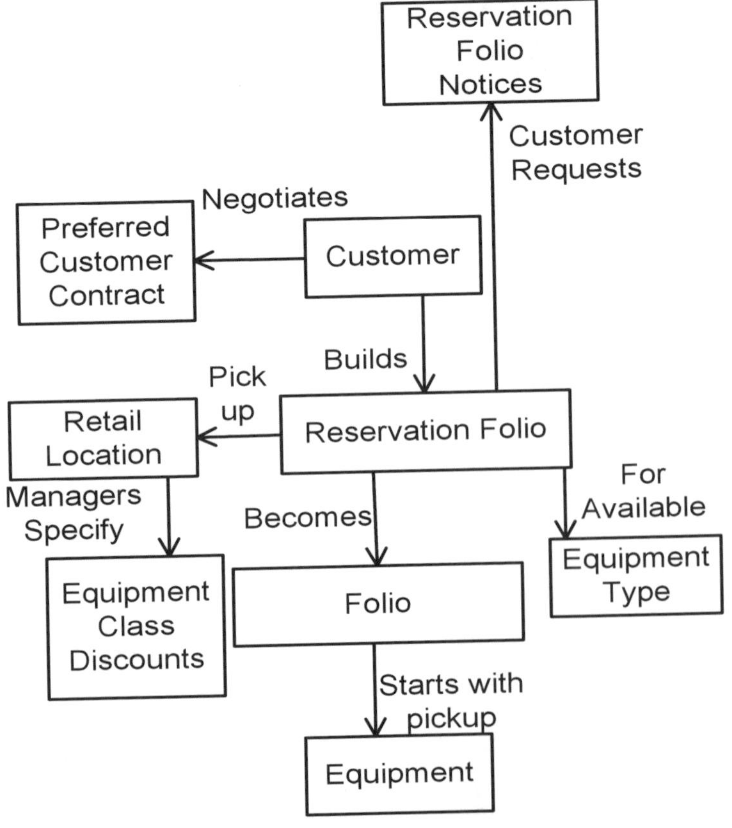

Figure 4.5 The Customer Business Rules need to find the customer's discounts and notify the customer about equipment availability when the reservation is placed.

For the Customer Discount Business Rule, the information we need must identify the customer's discount and the equipment class discounts. The customer discount is part of the negotiated contract for a preferred customer. The equipment type discounts are associated with a retail location. The manager offers discounts to lower his excess inventory.

If customers reserve an equipment type that is unavailable, then the reservation folio might report other available equipment. Whether or not the customer uses the feature, the notice should be logged every time a customer requests unavailable equipment. Management uses this information to decide if more equipment is needed at retail store.

These data ideas identify the input data types for the discount business rules. A data type definition expresses a simple record type in:

```
<?xml version="1.0" encoding="UTF-8"?>
<!ELEMENT customerDiscountRule (
CustomerId, reservationFolioId, discount)>
<!ELEMENT customerDiscountRule (#PCDATA)>
<!ELEMENT reservationFolioId (#PCDATA)>
<!ELEMENT discount (#PCDATA)>
```

These data concepts also identify the input data types for the notification business rules. A simple record type is expressed in a data type definition:

```
<?xml version="1.0" encoding="UTF-8"?>
<!ELEMENT customerNoticeRule (
CustomerId, reservationFolioId, onOff)>
<!ELEMENT customerDiscountRule (#PCDATA)>
<!ELEMENT reservationFolioId (#PCDATA)>
<!ELEMENT onOff (#PCDATA)>
```

These record types will be used in the business processes to connect the business rule to the web service.

Web Services for Business Rules

Web services use a client/server model. The business process is an example of a client, and the business rules engine is an example of a web service server.

Clients of web services interact with those web services through port types and operations. A port type is the name of the entry point for the service; like a virtual doorway. Attached to each port type are optional inbound data (input) and optional outbound data (output). Web services support many different port types. These comprise:

- One-Way: only input
- Request-Response: only output

- Solicit-Response: input and output
- Notice: only output.

Business rules should use the Solicit-Response port type. The business rule has input (request) and output (reply). Information is input for confirmation. Business rules output provides three types of output: valid or invalid, transformed data and error messages.

Figure 4.6 explains how the business process runs the business rule in the rules engine as a client to a service binding server. On the server, the port type, *DiscountRule* has an operation called *Validate*. In the BPEL engine, the process assigns values to the customer identifier and the reservation identifier.

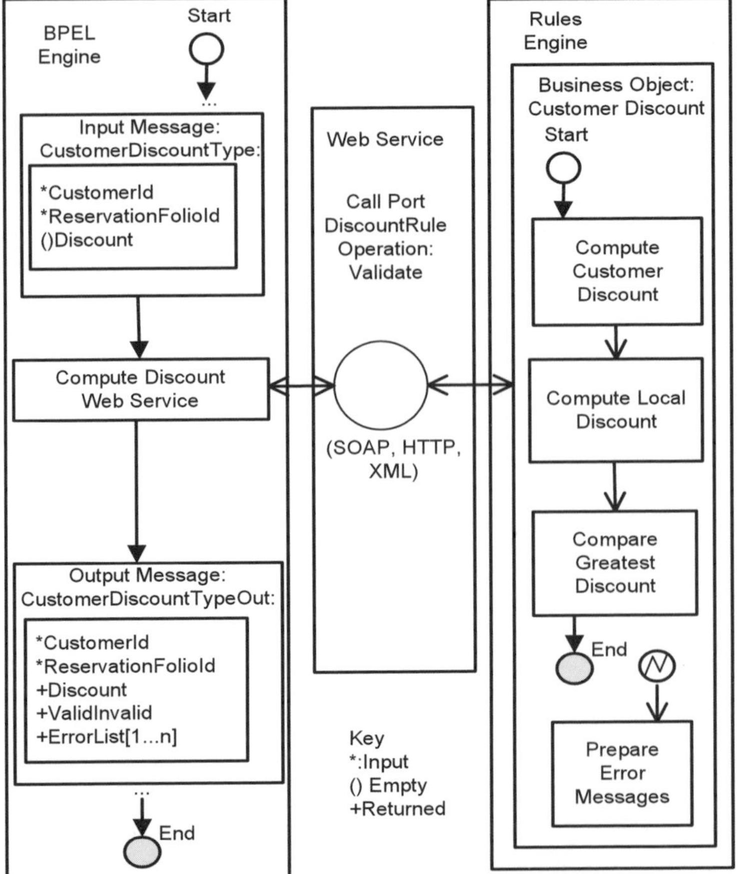

Figure 4.6 The web service for the customer discount uses the input data to apply the business rule and return the proper discount.

The business rules engine consumes the data and then runs through the computations, comparisons and controls; finally returning values. If no errors occur, the value returned is the customer discount and the field *Valid* set to *true*. If there are errors, for instance the rule could not match a customer identifier with a record, then the field *Valid* is set to *false* and error messages are returned.

The following fragment of the specification details how a WSDL would specify the port and operation for the scenario shown in figure 4.6.

```
<wsdl:portType name="DiscountRule">
 <wsdl:operation name="validate">
 <wsdl:input message="inputCustomerDiscount"/>
  <wsdl:output message="outputCustomerDiscountType"/>
 </wsdl:operation>
</portType>
<wsdl:message name="inputCustomerDiscount">
 <wsdl:part name="in0" type="tns2:customerDiscount"/>
</wsdl:message>
<wsdl:message name="inputCustomerDiscount">
 <wsdl:part name="in0" type="tns2:customerDiscountout"/>
</wsdl:message>
```

Again, the advantage to the web service is that you can change the computer program the port and the operation calls while avoiding changes to the client—the business process. Procedural code is inside the business rules engine, working out the details that we designed when we created the business rule.

Architecturally, the business process or application does not encase the business rules. Rather, the web service treats the business rule like a procedural call from a computer language. This is why web services and business processes interact well with business rules. The business rules software publishes a rule for, let's say, a customer or employee policy, and many different systems can use that same rule. With the loosely connected architecture described here, a constraint, policy or computational change often will not affect the process itself. Unless the input record changes, you change underlying computations and reference data with no impact to the web service.

Business Rules and the Business Object

In figure 4.6, the business object puts into effect the business rule. A business object is an object (in this case, the customer discount object) that contains all the attributes, records and computations that carry out the policy or constraint goals. Sometimes a business object runs a business use case creates a *business transaction,* which is a part of the long running transaction of the business process.

Business rules repositories usually have either an engine or an application generator that use metadata or business rules respectively to produce computer code. Either approach enforces the basic constraints, policies and doctrine of the enterprise. The code creates a bridge or a deductive connection from the business rule to the process.

Adding Business Rules to the Business Process

Once the business rules team generates, or publishes, the web service, the business process team adds the rule. Most BPM software has utilities that make this task simple. The BPM software should read the WSDL and create data types for the input and output.

For each of the processes that use a web service, there are a few extra steps you will need to take. You should map the form attributes of the business process to the input of the service. Your mapping may need some conversions, such as converting numbers to strings and strings to dates.

The process team will need to decide what to do if the business rule fails, and what to do with error messages.

In Figure 3.6, in the last chapter, I presented the customer relationship process. The process team might set up the business rule for the customer as a subprocess as follows:

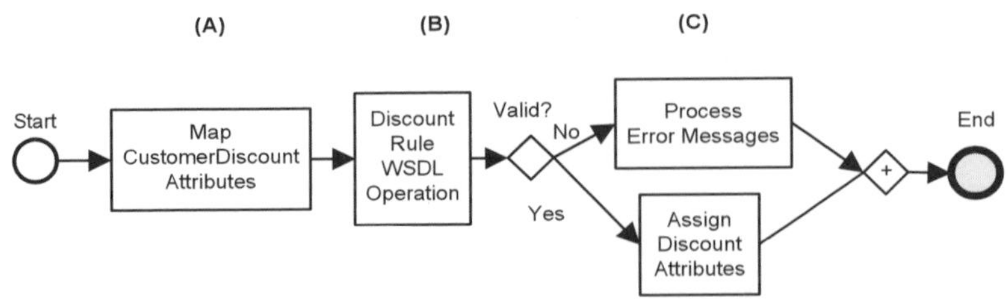

Figure 4.7 The web service for the customer discount might be implemented as a subprocess.

In step (A), the process maps the customer identifier and the location identifier to the input for the web service. In step (B) the process calls the web service operation. In step (C), the process either encounters an error or maps a discount to the output of the service.

Summary of Business Rules Concepts

In a BPM/BR project, the business processes are responsible for the flow of data that is fed into the business rules. The business rules activity defines and manages the content of application transactions, collaborative transformations, systems procedures and other rules. These might include business to business processes. Core processes use the business form developed by your organization. You use the Business Rules Approach to map this form to a record needed by the ERP packages. This is called creating a canonical, or basic, form. The details of the exchange of information can be isolated from changes to the ERP package.

Business rules also:

- Define measures and dimensions for construction of fact schemas in the data warehouse
- Inspect or report metrics and dimension ranges across aggregated data. This will be covered in the next chapter.
- Carry out directed, short lived special offerings. This is a key feature of CRM. We suggested this in our customer discount rule. Because the BPM/BR positions the application for change, it can carry out short-term product campaigns, time and availability limitations.
- Permit exceptions to hard and soft rules, allow customers and trading partners to bypass procedures, prevent invalid interactions.

The process for developing business rules is dependent on the project's nature. Since organizations use the BPM/BR for creating a combination of integrations, operational systems or data warehouses, each process will be slightly different. For instance, if attributes are to be transformed for an ERP, then business rules are the result of mapping those attributes. If the organization is developing policies for financing customer purchases, then the management team needs to develop these rules in a collaborative way.

Classes of Business Rules

The simplest part of the business rule is the statement of a term. In a business rules project, an early step is to collect all the needed terms. Collectively, terms define singular, high-level ideas. When the analysis changes the term into various flavors and types, they trigger a special subset of business rules.

For instance, a contract might be a term; then a fixed-fee contract becomes a modified term. A customer might be a term; a foreign customer becomes a modified term. Each of these data classifications classifies business rules.

The computations in business rules build on modified terms. For instance, some rules might look-up or transform record attributes. A rule might need to query a customer's data from a credit card number. Another rule's query might recall payment terms for an invoice from the contract number. When this happens, these subtypes apply to more business rules.

A business rule controls with redline values such as constraints, minimum or maximum conditions. Such values invoke other rules or control something in a business process. Control might override prior choices or control decisions based on time durations. Because business rules apply the same way to any process that uses it, they are an excellent way to state and enforce policies.

For instance, a factory order is a *long running transaction* affecting many different systems. As the business processes runs, business rules act on the cumulative transaction. Business rules work with business forms compared with data models. A business rule jumps from field to field on the business form. The business rule's data hierarchy is like a paper business form over the entities of a data model. A data model contains many different business cases. A business form is a single business case.

Different organization can call the same idea by different names. In the BPM/BR, we call these aliases. They might even have different values mapped across these aliases; applying the policies and constraints of that organization and cutting out the stovepipe disconnection (an important aim of EAI). The rules of the discipline, say accounting compared with manufacturing, instantiate their own semantically correct version of the rules.

A business rule positions the details of the idea for global changes. Policies are often about the timely reporting of accounting data, process connections, and available resources. If changes result from analysis such as economic analysis, Business Intelligence, responses to the competitive environment, or government regulations and laws, then the enterprise can easily change the rule.

Summary

Clear business rules supported by a robust business process make everyone's life easier.

The results of the business rules analysis activity are the goals, data dictionary and entries in the business rules tool. The output is also the connection of the business rules engine to the business process.

BPM tools easily build applications that manage the streams of business forms. They are excellent for managing the *when* and *where* of a business scenario. Processes automatically route data to the correct system. Yet it is easy to put too much application code in a BPM tool, especially if this code, the stuff we want to specify in business rules, is going to change. Simplistically, I call this the *why* part of the business. For instance, you might develop a complex loan qualification process that calls data from database tables and web services. If it is constantly changing, then I would suggest that this be one process activity that should call a business rule web service.

When the BPM/BR team uses a business rules analysis to discover, analyze and group the business rules, they are supporting a tree-like structure of decisions, policies and constraints for the business. Examples include the best source for a requisition, or when to salvage a fixed asset. Policies might include who is qualified for a loan. The branches of the tree start with the statement of a term and become more complex as the rule uses the term in records and computations. Business rules specify constraints, or redline values. These are the minimum or maximum conditions to invoke other rules, override low-level choices or decide the time duration for a condition.

Our aim is to be able to maintain process and procedures separately from the validations of decisions. Business Rules Sentences are themselves loosely connected to the architecture through the web interfaces. Structurally, a business rule positions an idea for rapid, global change.

If you intend to create a composite application, then you will probably need composite business rules. Information comes from many sources in the service oriented architecture. It is important to set up loose binding among the origins of the validation data needed by the rules. You might use services to separate technical details from reference data or transactions from implementation—you might change the source of the data without changing the business rule and without changing the process.

Business rules are associated with and affect transactional data exchanges and business events. Business rules uniquely specify a corporate use of the business process. In other words, special practices and tactics are put into effect in the business rules.

Here are the bullets that you should take away from this chapter:

- Business rules classify, compute, compare and control data to direct the flow in a business process.
- Business rules can certify the data in the business forms.
- When developing your business rules, you should write out the goal of the business rule in simple English.
- The goal should suggest the data you need and the computation that should be performed.
- The Business Rules Approach builds a dictionary of business terms. These terms include labels for computations.
- The business rules software publishes the business rule in terms of a web service.

CHAPTER FIVE

Business Intelligence

Effective executive leadership solves problems large and small. In Sumter Rents, suppose a bulldozer lays unused because of the indolence of some employees. Someone has not ordered a critical spare part. Can you find the little circumstances in your business that adds up to big costs? Are there glitches in the operations and processes that your employees could easily correct?

Looking at the big picture, managers use Business Intelligence (BI) to evaluate the condition or performance of their areas of responsibility with key performance indicators and other metrics. With BI, you create a system that pictures these metrics with a dashboard: speedometers, gauges, and box-and-whisker plots. When a particular measure is out of range, the manager easily drills into the underlying data to discover the issues and the problems.

The dashboard monitors standard productivity measures—such as cost of sales, inventory turnover, and others. With a business process approach, the dashboard also oversees the efficiency of process execution. A process performs at a particular speed and each step takes time. By combining business metrics and process performance, we arrive at a new understanding: business activity monitoring

Business Intelligence can hold data and computations that are in business processes and business rules engines. Managers use BI to identify the rules and processes that contribute to poor (or outstanding) performance.

BI has a role to play in the service oriented architecture. Imagine metrics that ferret out poorly performing products at a retail store. With a web service and a composite application, you could send reports to the managers responsible for the product, suspend shipments from the manufacturer and alert the purchasing agent Most BI vendors provide web services interfaces to their environments that assist in this process.

Business Intelligence aids executive decisions and business monitoring with data warehousing. Organizations, like Sumter Rents, oversee their performance with Business Intelligences (BI). Increasingly, government and industry use BI to strengthen their decision processes. Their aim is to understand and identify what factors affect productivity or performance metrics. Business Intelligence depicts performance with a simple dashboard of thermometers, gauges, speedometers and other widgets. When the dashboards are driven by current information, BI becomes Business Activity Monitoring (BAM). With the BI approach, a manager is only a few mouse clicks away from the detailed data that powers the dashboard's features.

The BI dashboard insulates users from the complexities of a database. A BI dashboard consists of:

- Display controls that depict metrics through a managed query environment (MQE). This allows non-technical analysts to examine the data behind the metrics. The user can customize the focus of the metrics.
- A data warehouse of information that compiles the metrics for the dashboard, and monitors and stores the details of the computations.
- An MQE repository that stores queries, details of graphical screens and report presentations. The repository controls security for users, and groups of users.

The promise of the BI environment is that managers will get an expressive representation of the information that models their business. This allows even non-technical managers to gain insights into complex business operational trends. They will spend a large part of their time analyzing data: fully aware of subtle shifts in the business environment. The BI approach will eclipse the efforts of specialized data analysts. The manager will be able to progressively dissect a metric in a business circumstance. For instance, if a retail store is consistently underperforming in one area, managers use BI to identify this problem and adjust the causes.

To create a BI environment, your team should build an analytical data warehouse for managers and other decision makers. The outcome of a BI project should be a creative, exploratory tool.

In many enterprises, important decision making metrics are scattered across a diverse landscape of systems. This is why Business Process Management is a powerful way of gathering this data. Combining data warehousing and BPM provides a method to integrate the disparate stovepipes of information.

The team's earlier effort in business processes and business rules will support the analysis needed for creating BI. Business rules helps to define the dimensions and measures. The trick is to use the analysis of BPM and BPM/BR to provide the information needed to enhance the data schema for the data warehouse.

Hardee's used Business Intelligence to create their successful, albeit over the top, product the Monster Burger.

Strategic Business Intelligence for Sumter Rents

Sumter Rents' income comes from leasing equipment. Naturally, Sumter's accountants and business managers have developed rental rates for every equipment type in their inventory. As we will see, the important assumption in their rate computation is the number of days the equipment will be leased over the life of the equipment. Eventually, customer rental sales are volume is proportional to Sumter's inventory.

Since equipment leasing is Sumter's core business, creating and restocking a quality inventory is a fundamental, budgeted part of this activity. Also, Sumter's customers enjoy the convenience, safety and efficiency of the new models.

Unlike automobiles, much of Sumter's aged fleet of bulldozers, cranes, motorized lifts, and other heavy equipment, keeps significant marketplace value. Much of new equipment funding is the capital from the sales of existing inventory. Recently, overseas markets have put upward pressure on the prices of used equipment.

In previous years, Sumter has haphazardly sold a portion of the existing inventory. Because there is a high demand for quality used construction equipment, the managers of Sumter aim to plan their sales and new purchases using a Business Intelligence system. When Sumter buys and sells equipment it is adjusting its rental inventory. Overall, Sumter managers know they need a more surgical approach. The challenge is to choose the ideal number of units to buy and sell by matching the rental inventory to customer demand.

The Business Intelligence team meets with the managers from almost every division of Sumter Rents. There were many issues discussed. Among these were:

- How do we improve sales projections?
- What is the cost of restocking the leasing capacity?
- How do we avoid selling too much inventory, or selling it too late?

What came of these meetings was a consensus that rental inventory should be better planned. A balance is needed between revenue from used equipment sales, new capital investment and projected rental sales. The analysis should be a combination of statistics and Business Intelligence.

The goal is a best fit between inventory and customer demand. To develop projections of customer demand, the Business Intelligence team will need to assemble, store and analyze detailed rental sales data. If this information is timely, it will become a powerful analytical and monitoring tool that provides insights into Sumter's performance. Further, managers will be able to pay closer attention to the many details and trends of the business.

The *Engineering News Record* publishes regional construction activity indexes which predict construction activity. This is used to predict changes in the demand for Sumter's heavy equipment. Sumter managers plan to perform a multivariate regression analysis of their demand against this data.

Sumter Rents aims to develop a preferred customer program to build loyalty with their largest customers. So, if the rental sales information includes customer data, then the BI environment should be able to identify those customers.

A Process for Business Intelligence in BPM/BR

Figure 5.1 presents a business process for developing Business Intelligence for the BPM/BR project.

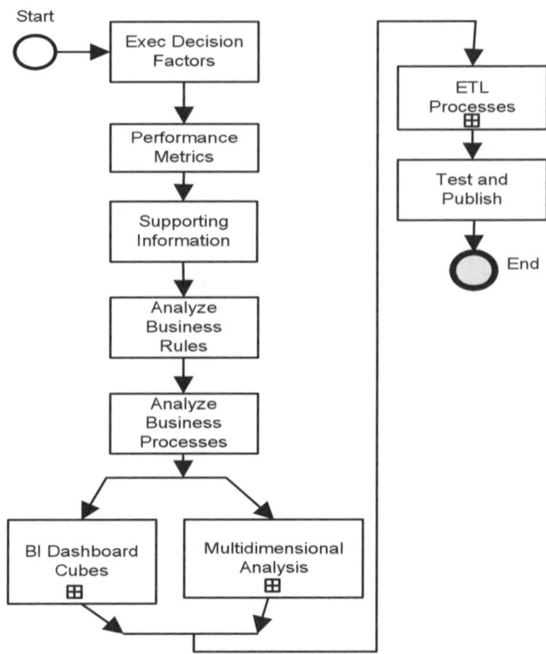

Figure 5.1 This is a basic process for developing Business Intelligence for the project.

The first step is to develop the factors for executive decisions: How does top management evaluate business activity performance? In general terms, what are the metrics or key performance indicators for the business activity?

To carry out Business Intelligence, you will need to develop performance metrics that are relevant to the business activity. The project team will need to research and approve a proposed method of computing the metrics. The computations use information they gathered. At this phase, as a prelude to creating the manager's performance dashboard, the formula will be a specification that data designers use to verify their model.

The next step is to identify the topics, entities and events needed to support the decisions. An entity might be a customer or one unit of equipment. Events are: equipment purchase, a customer lease or a customer return and maintenance. This step is a prelude to loading the data warehouse and performing data analysis.

The BI team will need to explore business rules for the relevant business activity. Business rules define important redline values (limits and constraints) that should be a part of the details that managers see in the queries.

Business process software collects time duration data for processes. The team should dissect business processes for performance and other factors that would be useful for the manager's analysis.

The team develops prototypes of the BI Dashboard and underlying cubes. At the same time, they develop the multidimensional data structures. Figures 5.2 and 5.3 present these subprocesses.

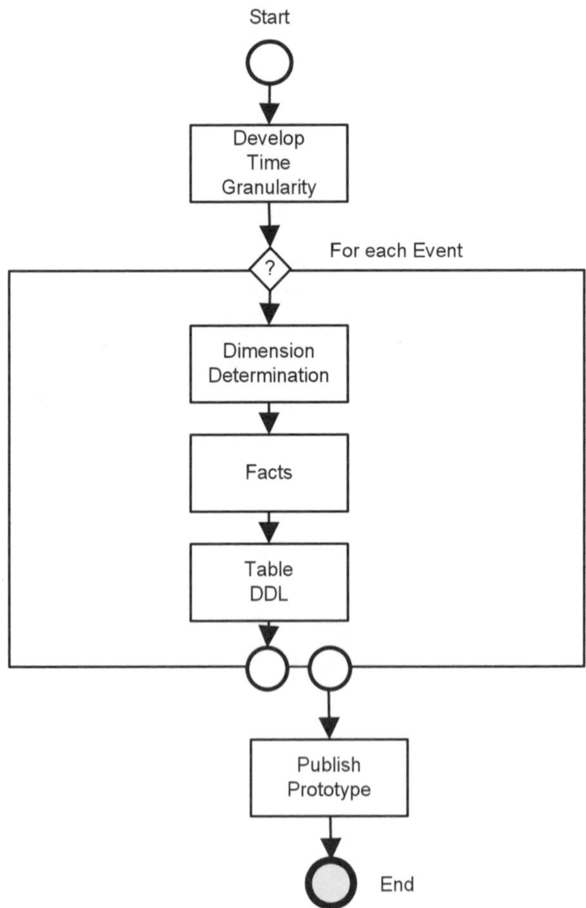

Figure 5.2 This is the multidimensional analysis subprocess.

Metrics and key performance indicators are aggregate measurements of the facts associated with one or more events (orders, sales, or receipts) or financial accounts. In multidimensional analysis, the Business Intelligence team builds a table layout that the query environment uses to compute the metrics. First, they select a time granularity - or slice of time - for the ETL process to aggregate the data. For instance, if metrics need monthly data, then ETL condenses daily data into a month format.

Next, the BI team adds dimensions to the facts so metrics are computed to various levels of detail. For instance, if a metric is about a retail store, then the team is likely to add higher dimensions of city, state and sales region. In general, they start with a physical layout (DDL) of the tables in the source systems. An analysis of business rules might reveal dimensions that are not obvious by looking at the source data structures alone. Also, business processes may have useful timing information about steps.

After the team models facts they build a table layout (DDL). This is the physical design of the data structure. They might build a rapid prototype and populate it with sample data. This is useful for the executive dashboard or scorecard development.

When the team builds the dashboard or scorecard, they select a fitting widget for the executive metric. The selection is based on the monitoring imagery you need. Monitoring might include trends, key performance indicators, correlations, thresholds and others. Examples include the *thermometer* and the *box and whisker*. These might include limits on target values and current values. Widgets may depict a warning symbol to stand for a serious condition that the manager needs to explore. The manager controls the level at which the metric is computed—company wide, sales region, state and others.

For each of the widgets, the designers design *cubes* that reveal the data that supports the metric. This is where the user might *slice and dice* the facts behind the metric. In this process, a user searches for the critical information that reveals underperformance.

Besides executive metrics, BI environments produce standardized reports. The MQE software pushes reports to decision makers and managers.

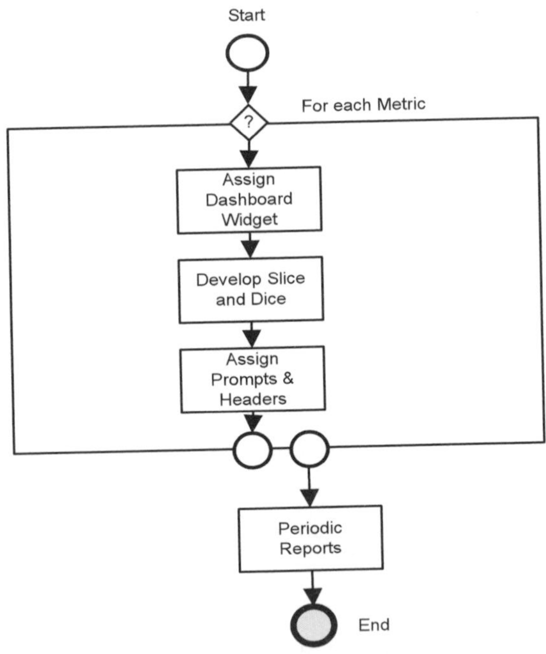

Figure 5. 3 This is a process for developing the executive dashboard.

The extraction, translation and load (ETL) process populates and updates information in the tables. I have shown this as a subprocess because your design team should do this with a business process (chapter 3). If there are several source systems, then you might need to encode common value dimensions. By encoding, I mean the ETL process converts codes and lists to a single standard. This translation is well suited to a Business Rules Approach. Some Business Process vendors have added ETL abilities to their product suites that automate the process of building data warehouse records from many sources.

In the last step of a BI process, the team will certify the result. The executive metrics should be confirmed with data and management review. Finally, the BI system is published for use by decision makers.

BI and data warehousing has been around for years. Data warehouses are built to spew out mounds of data. However, what executives and managers need is data in context of how the business is performing. You should include data that affects the conduct of dealings with a customer or other productive task. Managers are already measuring some of this. If something is underperforming, then this information provides insights.

Business Intelligence Concepts

Business Intelligence Concepts are included in Figure 5.4.

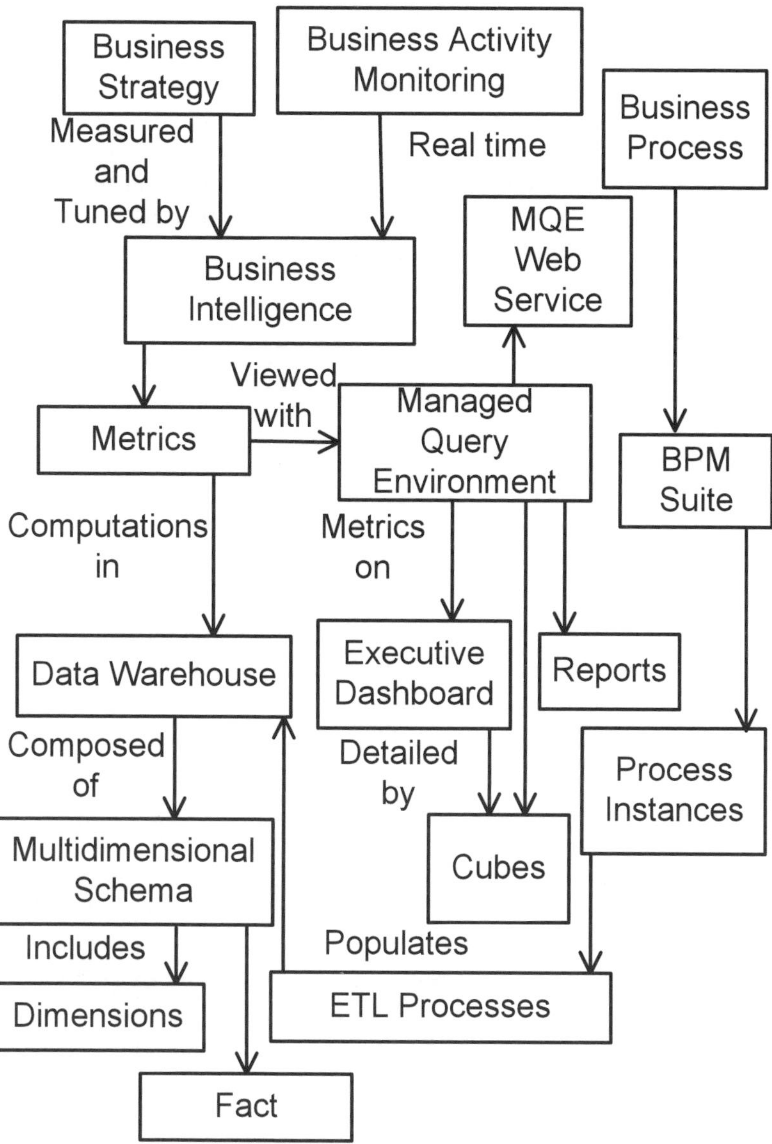

Figure 5.4 This is the concept diagram for Business Intelligence.

Business Intelligence is an umbrella term for a set of concepts and methods to improve business decision making by using a fact based system. Business Intelligence supports business strategy by creating a tool for measuring and tuning the outcome.

A metric is a formula of one or more facts that is useful for managers to decide or check the health of an area of responsibility. For a data warehouse to be a Business Intelligence system, it must provide consequential metrics. An example in our case study might be the percentage of target leasing days for a specific month and a given equipment type.

The data warehouse is a set of database tables that hold the dimensions and facts, the MQE, and the processes that populate and manage the data.

A multidimensional data schema is a set of data that has been designed to compute summaries of facts according to many dimensions for a needed time. For instance, Sumter sales revenue might be totaled for the company, by a region, an equipment type, or many others. The data is designed for dashboard users to look for trends and outstanding information.

A dimension is a holder of descriptive detail, including types, categories, or named entities from the business ideas. Examples of a dimension from the Sumter Business case are: equipment types, maintenance types, sales division. Examples of *named entities* would be a customer, a store or a reservation.

A fact is a numeric attribute that is associated with a dimension. Facts are also called measures. Examples are quantity, size, and time duration.

A Managed Query Environment (MQE) is a suite of software that provides user-friendly, easy access to the dimensions, facts and metrics. Examples are Cognos™ and BusinessObjects™. Business Intelligence happens when you use these tools to support the executive decisions.

The executive™ dashboard is a graphical presentation of metrics that support decisions.

A cube refers to the mapping between the data that stores the facts and dimensions, and the information that describes the prompts and column headings (*metadata*). The cube is a user-friendly connection between a manager's point-and-click and the technical query. The cube might supply facts that support the dashboard.

Software vendors use the cube term for a collection of user selectable objects that direct a query access to a source of data. Users look at the cube when they need to see a slice of data behind a dashboard control. The cube is a collection of data definitions, relationships, and other symbols that are stored in the BI repository. MQE software controls user access to the cube with security features.

The MQE vendors provide web services that work with other products in your architecture to can produce important decision reports. Often the result of BI is the push of key findings to managers.

Many MQE vendors provide web services that work with other products in your architecture. With BI web services you extend and customize business processes and business rules. Also MQE web services extend and customize reporting products.

Decision Factors for Sumter

To plan for the ideal inventory, we need to develop basic inventory metrics for the rental processes. The executives decide on the size of the rental inventory based on a projection of the annual demand. Management matches inventory with demand for several quarters. In discussions with management these causes where noted:

- Excessive inventory leads to fewer days of rentals per unit.
- Inadequate inventory lessens sales and increases overhead allocated to the equipment.
- Demand varies from season to season.

Simple accounting decides the basic rental charge for equipment. Sumter accountants base the rental charge on the total cost of ownership plus an allocation of overhead and the age of ownership. So given these numbers:

- a unit costs $100K, including overhead,
- history tells us customers will lease the equipment 60% of the time,
- the margin is 10%,
- Equipment life is 48 months.

The daily charge for the equipment should be $126/Day. Let's call the percentage of days in lease—the Target Leasing Rate (TLR). Preferred customers increase the profit because they lease equipment for longer periods of time. This is the rational for their negotiated discounts.

Once accounting has set up a rental fee for equipment, managers should oversee the total leasing rates. Leasing rates will predictably vary from season to season, so the BI system will need to compensate this.

There are many different equipment types and equipment costs. The prices for a single equipment type increases yearly. Because it would not be popular to be constantly changing the rental fee, Sumter should rarely change the TLR.

Customers might rarely lease large expensive equipment, while ordinary bulldozers and motorized lifts may have high target leasing rates.

As I mentioned earlier, construction equipment keeps significant value. So each equipment type has a target age: the best time to salvage the equipment, based on a combination of the tax benefits, and the retail value. So even if customers demand remains constant, a certain number of units will need to be replaced.

Here are the decision metrics that BI will model:

- The target leasing rate, an aggregate percentage of the number of days equipment is leased to a customer.
- Actual leasing rate, the annualized percentage of the leasing rate, computed for Sumter sales data, this equates to an aggregate of customer demand.

You might also view these rates as the efficiency of the leasing process. A value of 1.0 would mean customer have leased every equipment unit.

Performance Metrics for Sumter

Organizations are successful with Business Intelligence when they develop the goals and objectives that match executive decisions. The objective of Sumter's BI systems is to contribute to the profitability by steering the company towards the correct inventory. Because the economics that create rental demand change from quarter to quarter, an ideal inventory is impossible to achieve. Yet, Sumter wants to know where to set the inventory and how fast to get there.

Managers oversee business activities by comparing measurements of current activities against target, or baseline measurements. The TLR is Sumter's baseline metric for monitoring rental inventory. The equation for the target lease rate for a population of equipment is:

$$TLR = SAF*(((TCO+ Overhead) / Daily rental Fee)/ Target Age)$$

Where

- SAF = the seasonal adjusted factor, an integral of the seasonal adjustment factors for leasing rate
- Total Cost of Ownership (TCO)= The total cost of ownership including purchase, maintenance, licenses and other fees
- Overhead = the overhead allocated to the equipment unit, usually a percentage of the TCO.

- Daily rental fee, the assigned fee for the equipment type.
- Target age is the planned salvage age of the equipment, in days.

During analysis, MQE software sums this formula for the equipment and chosen time range. The formula adjusts the target lease rate throughout the year. So the software estimates daily changes in demand with a regression of sales data. For instance, different holidays, which have low leasing activities, will adjust the target lease rate. When the BI software computes the metric it also computes the SAF in the analysis period.

The cost of rental for the equipment varies by customer and retail store. Preferred customers boost the leasing rate by leasing more equipment for longer periods of time. To improve leasing rates, store managers offer discounts during seasonally slow periods.

Managers evaluate the rental activity performance by comparing the target rate against rental sales. A formula computes the actual lease rate (ALR):

ALR = (Total Leasing Days)/Number of Units

Where

- Total Leasing Days = the days the unit was assigned to a paying customer.
- Number of units = total number in the analysis.

The BI team will design the data warehouse to be able to support these computations for any useful combinations of equipment types, customers, sales areas and time boundaries.

Information Needed for Sumter's Inventory Management System

The Sumter's BI supports inventory decisions through an evaluation of the two metrics: Target Leasing Rate and Actual Leasing Rate. Executives will use these metrics to evaluate the rental inventory levels.

The metric formulas need information from different systems in Sumter Rents. Figure 5.5 displays the needed information.

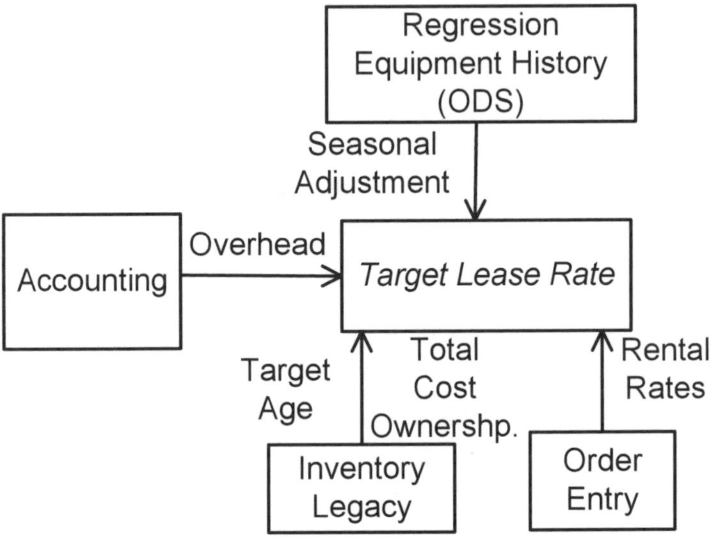

Figure 5.5 This is the concept diagram for Business Intelligence.

The BI team studied the sources of the information and decided:

- Rental Days assigned to customers is available from the equipment history data described in Chapter 3. A regression of the data develops the seasonal adjustment factors.
- The formulas also need rental rates for the equipment. The Sumter Order entry system maintains the prices for equipment rental. There are two rental rates: the retail rate and the rate assigned to the customer. The TLR needs the retail rental rate.
- The overhead for the TCO comes from an account in the general ledger. Since cost and salaries vary, the overhead varies.
- The formulas need the total cost of ownership (TCO) and the salvage age of the equipment. These data are available from a legacy system.

Similarly, the assigned leasing rate is computed from information in the operational data store.

The executive dashboard needs more than facts or numbers. It uses dimensions to focus on different parts of the business. Besides the entire business, the managers will want to look at metrics for a sales region, an equipment type, or a store. Also, the managers will want to look at the metrics across different time boundaries—last quarter compared with the current, last year compared this, and others.

The dimensions gathered from different systems should be converted to one standard. The dimensions that span several application systems need data standardization. The BI team creates a uniform dimension set that are semantically correct and supports the business model.

In this information gathering task, the BI team identifies the different systems contributing to the business model. The ETL processes get data for the business model. For each of the systems, one or more ETL processes might be needed. This analysis verifies what dimensions and facts that will be provided by the ETL process.

Considering Business Rules

Earlier, I described business rules as composed of categories, computations comparisons and controls. Business Intelligence should incorporate this information into the data explored in the executive dashboard's cube.

Business rules are often designed to influence customer and trading partner behavior. Managers use BI to verify the effect. For example, special customer discounts should increase the equipment lease duration. Sumter offers corporate customer discount to large companies with long leases. Business Intelligence discovers these customers. BI also continues to measure leases after the discount is negotiated.

Some business rules are designed to influence customer and trading partner behavior, and managers can use BI to verify the effect.

A theme of Business Intelligence, as carried out by the executive dashboard, is to monitor the big picture metrics. When performance is poor, look for parts of the business that under perform and search for incidents, trends and patterns that cause the poor performance.

To incorporate business rules into your Business Intelligence, you should:

1. Identify rules that affect the metrics you are modeling,
2. Analyze the rule for redline values, incorporate these as dimensions in the data warehouse (customers with good credit, accepted quality measures, and others),
3. Extract numerical computations and add these as facts in the data warehouse.

If you build your Business Intelligence system with these considerations, then your managers will be able to evaluate the effects of changing redline values and computations.

This is another reason for using Business Rules Approach. Because rules are centralized, it is simple to find the rules and use them to evaluate the decisions.

Considering Business Processes

The equipment process logs location changes in the database. There are details about customer leasing, scheduled maintenance and the time on the retail store lot. Between these, there are steps that take place. Store personnel prepare equipment for customer use, inspect equipment returned from the customer, and maintain the equipment.

We have three simple motions in the equipment. The basic system work flow consists of:

1. The customer places a reservation for equipment. The equipment manager should prepare the equipment for the customers before they arrive to pick up the equipment. The reservation process records the scheduled pickup time and the equipment process records the time of customer assignment.
2. The customer returns the equipment. The ordering process records the drop-off time. The equipment process records when an employee enters the equipment inspection form.
3. The equipment process tells the managers when they should maintain the equipment. The equipment manager performs the maintenance and records this data.

Business process suites write logs of the dates and time of these activities. These are just three of the essential time records that should be watched. The BI team might add these time slices to the data elements in the data warehouse.

When your team builds a data warehouse in a business process environment, they should consider adding process scheduling data to identify other business events. The requirements of the business model will dictate the event definition. For instance, in an order entry process, if we analyze shipping and receiving, then some events may have occurred, such as the time between the order and a series of receipts.

To incorporate business process timing and performance into the data warehouse you should:

1. Identify process activities that are connected to the business activity you are monitoring.

2. Find the source of timing records for the steps.
3. Incorporate the date or time variances into the data warehouse.

Business Intelligence Dashboard

With the right combination of displays and controls, the BI team creates an executive dashboard that rapidly oversees developments at Sumter Rents. They should create a vision of the characteristics of a business monitoring environment: what managers see and how they interact with the analysis space. If the system is difficult to use, misleading, or filled with uncomfortable semantics, then it will not be well received.

When designing an executive dashboard, the team chooses between dimension-based and measure-based controls. Because Sumter has many retail stores in many states, the team might use a map to allow the manager to select inventory metrics form several categories. The dashboard allows dimension-based controls when the manager wants to drill up and down. In drilling, managers use cubes to explore the multidimensional business model. So managers might want to see heavy crane lease rates in several states, then they might want to see heavy crane rental in the entire enterprise.

A dimension-based dashboard has one or more dimensions and one or more measures. There are almost always at least two metrics in a control: a target or baseline value and often also a historical value. When the historical value is above or below the baseline value then managers need to discover the performance issues. This is where they drill into details and slice and dice the information.

The managers choose dimensions in the executive dashboard then select which metrics to compute from the executive dashboard. When they drill to the cubes, they explore the records. For instance, suppose rentals in Virginia are below the seasonally adjusted factor for the current month. The manager slices and sorts the details, perhaps sorting on poorly performing stores. If there are no poorly performing stores, the manager sorts by equipment type. The manager continues this activity until they understand why the conditions exist.

In another scenario, a Business Intelligence system might use measure-based widgets to show the status of one measure alone, or compare several measures. For example, you might create a measure-based stoplight dashboard to show the status of one measure, or a measure-based gauge dashboard to compare several measures.

Measure-based dashboards do not always need a dimension. In such cases, the measures are totals for all dimensions in cube data sources. Because drilling is applicable only to dimensions, you cannot drill up and down on measure-based dashboards that do not plot a dimension.

Slice and Dice

The power of the cube is that the manager does not explore data with programming languages; the cube creates this for the user. The cube provides familiar business terms to the manager, not complex technical terms. The purpose is for users to think in sound business ideas and to be as easy to use as a dictionary.

As we mentioned, slice and dice and drill actions occur after the manager decides to explore a condition. Managers drill, or bring back data, from the widgets on the executive dashboard. For instance, a Sumter manager might discover poor rental sales in a state. The manager then drills to the detail. After this, they interact with the cube. In the slice and dice method of analysis, the manager uses tools to see data from different viewpoints and on different detail levels.

The aim of slice and dice is to analyze data by looking at it on different details and from contrasting viewpoints. Managers hope to gain ideas about the performance metrics and resolve problems. The cube provides explorations of information connections to the businesses events.

Cube data browsers have two modes: drill mode, and slice and dice mode. In slice and dice managers alternate the positions of data in a report. An important slice and dice capacity is to be able to pivot data tables or move data from columns to rows. Slice and dice mode also:

- Creates master-detail reports,
- Displays and selects data,
- Renames, resets and deletes blocks, and
- Changes tables and matrix tables into charts.

In the slice and dice mode, users edit table data, including break reports, filters, sorts, rankings, and statistics.

With a well-designed slice and dice layout, managers easily configure reports. They should be able to build a master-detail report and reorganize this report by reevaluating the master, or by revising a master-detail report.

The drill mode lets managers to get new data sets. The information in the slice and dice data creates the drill mode. For instance, after the manager selects a master detail report, the managers might revert to drill mode and reestablish other data items as master. Through a series of actions with the cube, the manager might need to explore another side of the data set—thus he or she might redefine the heading of the master report. For instance, suppose a manager discovers poorly performing equipment type at a store in the current month. The Sumter manager might drill across to other stores.

Cubes allow users to select various headings. For example, if the master header is the dimension "store," the user can replace it with "equipment type." In this way the user builds many master-detail reports. This query sequence enables the manager to see data on several detail levels.

Executive Dashboard Reports

Suppose Sumter Managers notice that retail stores neglect equipment on the lot, resulting in decreased leasing days reported on an item. With the cubes the BI team has created, MQE software sends reports to the store's equipment manager to address the problem.

There is an even more interesting development in the industry. With MQE web services, the BI team could incorporate complex conditions, involving many metrics into business processes and business rules.

Security

Security systems in the MQE software control access to the executive dashboard. Usually, local utilities briefly log the user onto the repository evaluate which cubes are available to the user. If a cube file is not present on the web server, it is imported. The user gets only the data they have access to.

Multidimensional Analysis

The dashboard needs data to compute the metrics, and managers need to see the details to explore the reasons for variances. The metrics will be computed with a query of the data for the part of the business the managers explore. The BI team provides the data by creating database tables to holds the information. Last, they create ETL processes to populate the data.

In multidimensional analysis, the team designs tables for events measured by the metrics. These tables become repositories of events and facts in the data warehouse. Also, these centralized structures might have details in associated, contemporaneous structures. Many dimensions are in the table structures.

For the inventory monitor, the key event is equipment location changes. The table is called the equipment fact table. It holds the state of equipment: either in the retail store, in maintenance or assigned to customers. There are several ways to design tables for the data warehouse. When the BI team designs this fact table, they group dimensions and facts into one data element. Information for equations is included in the same record of the fact table.

The easiest data warehouse table to build in the Sumter case would be a day-by-day log of:

- What store the equipments is assigned to,
- What state it is in: customer assigned, maintenance, or retail store lot,
- If it is assigned to a customer, then all the leasing data should be in the record, the lease, the customer and the rental rate.

If information for the equipment event is not contiguous in the needed form, then the ETL process will need to convert it to the data warehouse table.

Time dimensions should be associated with each of the records of the operational systems providing facts to the data warehouse. Facts and time dimensions include the customer leasing, retail store (idle), and the maintenance performed.

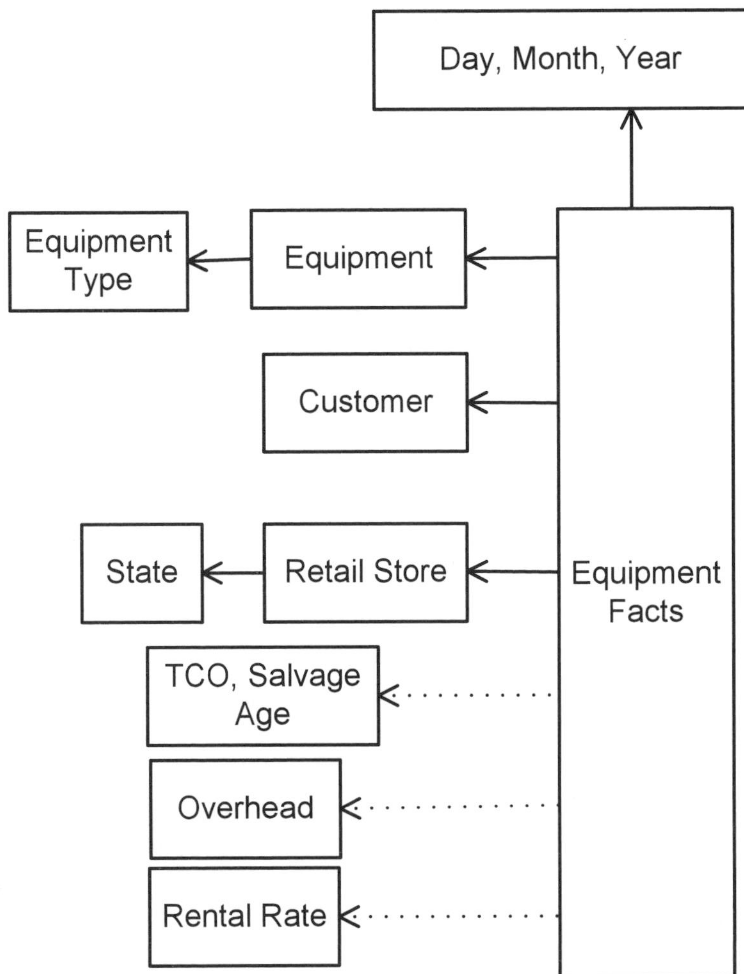

Figure 5.6 This is a simplified diagram of the equipment fact table. The diagram shows the contemporaneous nature of the records.

Figure 5.6 shows the equipment fact table. The solid arrows show dimension that are in the table. The dotted lines show facts copied from other systems into the table. Every equipment item has an entry for every day in the table. This allows the managers to explore metrics down to the individual equipment item. The top of the figure portrays the time dimension. The granularity of the equipment fact table must have enough detail to support the executive dashboard.

In interviews with managers, it is learned that there are two horizons to this objective. In the near view, managers study the leasing rate for the current month. In the longer view, managers evaluate the annual performance of Sumter.

An evaluation of the other records showed these findings:

- Equipment location is recorded daily.
- Statements of total cost of ownership, salvage age and overhead assets are available monthly.

When there is data for every piece of equipment, then not only do managers plan inventory for demand, they also find inefficiencies. Earlier I supposed that a bulldozer might sit idle for months with this data structure, managers will be able to discover this.

At this point, the BI team creates a rapid prototype of the fact structure.

ETL Processes

We have defined the dimension and measures for the model. We need to populate the data structures. Extraction Transform and Load (ETL) is the data processing activity of extracting data from diverse data sources, transforming the data, and then loading the data in a uniform format into a target data source. Your technical team might design and create the ETL programs, or you might use software to perform this work.

ETL is good to do with business process techniques. Because most ETL software automatically decides when to insert or update records. The software is also written to work with large record sets.

Earlier, the BI team identified sources of information for the equipment fact model. Our equipment fact table has dimensions and facts from four separate systems. Because management has decided to use the executive dashboard to do business activity monitoring, the data warehouse should have current data. The teams design a composite, real-time process to get these data. In a composite process one process gathers data across the systems.

The translation role of an ETL process might encode dimensions to one standard. For instance, we might have different equipment type codes in the legacy system than what is used in the operational data. The standard is the equipment types used in the operational data store. The ETL process standardizes the dimension.

ETL processes for getting the data may be:

- Batch extracts of the operational data, loading a flat file.

- Queries of the data through JDBC or middleware.
- Messages from another business process.

ETL processes sometimes need external sources of data. Subscribing to economic information could be a web service that is part of the process model.

BI Production

At first, the BI team might quickly prototype the Business Intelligence system with few automated processes. Programmers manually create, monitor and refresh the data warehouse. They manually correct process errors. As the project goes ahead, the programmers become a part of the solution set because they understand the ETL process. Their manual procedures become part of the computing infrastructure. For the analysts and management, this circumstance becomes undesirable because valuable resources become tied up in repetitious chores. When the ETL process is in production this circumstance is ended.

The final step of the BI project is production. The BI team has set up an executive dashboard that supports the project objectives. In production, the database needs to:

- Scale to a huge size,
- Report errors to the administrators,
- Perform large operations in parallel so maintenance and refreshes might be efficient and timely.

When the ETL processes load the data, the data warehouse has these characteristics:

- Process granularity: the ETL processes use isolated components that are executed in parallel.
- Process control: a process hierarchy is defined and controlled in the BPM suite.
- Intertask communications: the processes communicate with each other.
- Errors reported should controlled and broadcast.

In production, architectural components are "hardened" for use. Here the infrastructure is integrated through large-scale testing. Specific activities and deliverables include:

- Database server, tuned for optimum performance.
- Queries and views built during design are tested and tuned.
- Data warehouse distribution mechanisms are designed, configured, and tested.
- System backup procedures are put into effect and tested.

Much of the data in the data warehouse might hold sensitive information. Data might need to be withheld from groups of users. During construction, the MQE administrators create security groups and assigns users to these groups. The groups are limited to information that removes sensitive data from their view.

Testing

During quality assurance, or testing, the BI team should use a formal problem log that is available for the project leaders to review. This includes the problem area, suggested solution, responsible parties, and a suspense date for the correction. The project manager should review the problem log to discover trends and identify risks to the program.

Web Services for MQE

I have described how business processes use web services to carry out business rules. MQE vendors, such as Cognos™, provide web services interfaces to their systems. This gives the IT team a powerful way to add complex conditions into business rules and business processes.

With a web service interface, a process or rule responds to complex or subtle conditions in the business.

Business Intelligence is part of agile architecture—one that easily allows changes. Figure 5.8 suggests some of the features provided by combining web services in the agile architecture.

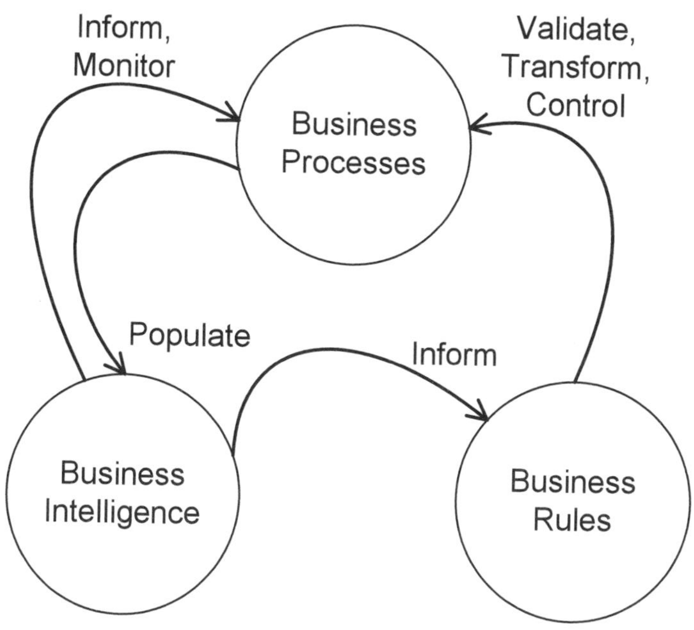

Figure 5.7 Web services and these technologies are essential to an agile architecture.

Figure 5.7 shows an extension of business processes, business rules and Business Intelligence. What is remarkable about these technologies is that there is an adaptable environment created with little traditional programming. When the Sumter technical team adds or changes a capability in one of these environments, they use modeling tools that model the business practice. The tools might be either a diagram of a business process, a business rule's goal or Business Intelligence metric or cube. The tools also create or use web services.

Publish and Act on the Results

Considering the dizzying array of circumstances builds a far-fetched case to optimize Sumter's rental inventory. The accountants have computed a target leasing rate for 700 types of equipment. There is a seasonal change to demand that complicates the speedometer widget on the BI panel. No wonder this was one of David Burk's (Chapter 2) chief business challenges. The momentum of the success that Sumter has had in the industry might lull the managers into complacency.

Implications are clear. Aging companies might use the legacy of their success to continue operations while ignoring the complexities needed to fine tune. Otherwise, they can use Business Intelligence to root out the inefficiencies and plan. The choice is clear: will you drive the numbers or will they drive you?

The key is creating a business structure drawn from the critical experiences of the operating past that provide the information for a better future. Second, the business environment is constantly changing in basic ways. The basics of economic theory are essential in every business, but the problems businesses face today are set in today's frameworks of beliefs, technologies, and radically lower information costs than ever before. The secret of success is creating efficient businesses that readily adapts to changing circumstances. BI creates these tools.

Summary

Here are the take away points of this chapter:

- Business Intelligence supports executive decisions. You use BI when the enterprise needs to oversee the total performance of the operation.
- Executive dashboards monitor historical and target metrics with expressive widgets such as speedometers, temperature gauges and stoplights.
- The data that creates the metric values should be available in cubes. Managers analyze cubes using slice, dice and drill.
- The tables that hold the data are developed with multidimensional analysis. In our example, we built a fact table that held all the dimensions needed in one row.
- Data are populated by extraction translation and loading processes. These processes are well suited for Business Process Management techniques described in Chapter 3.
- Business Intelligence Software has web services powers that extends business processes and business rules in novel ways.

References

Levinson, Meridith, 2004, "The Brain behind the Big Bad Burger and Other Tales Of Business Intelligence", CIO.

Kimball, Ralph, 1996, The Data Warehouse Toolkit, Wiley

CHAPTER SIX

IT Convergence

> Business Process management offers a powerful way to manage your legacy systems. If you have many legacy systems and many systems administrators, then there is a good chance that much of they do can be managed by BPM software
>
> To convert your legacy processes to a BPM environment, you should consider adding controls, error reporting and logging standards. This development effort is not extensive. The controls I suggest adding are the ones that your organization does manually.
>
> As you add support for legacy processes to business process management, you can start to add more capabilities to your environment.

There is an obvious place to consider using business process and business rules technology—look at the way your personnel manage systems and process data. After years of development, testing, and postproduction support, many enterprise information systems have become a myriad of processes, data loads, and extracts. These can become difficult to support. These processes feed commercial-off-the-shelf products (COTS), data warehouses and other parts of your technology stack. Many organizations are dependent on a team of technical personnel to oversee and control this complicated environment. The weights of these challenges complicate adding new capacities or improving service conditions for your users. In this environment, there is a driving need for an control of the processes that are accessible by nontechnical managers and administrators. BPM can meet this need.

BPM tools (Tibco™, SeeBeyond™ and WebMethods™) can used as a business integrated scheduling and control solution for data processes. Most BPM tools can offer web-based process controls that centralize all procedural business and data processing needs. This is called IT convergence. They do this with simple, consistent, applications. Through gateways BPM supports processes that are written in all types of languages, including Cobol, PL/SQL and Java, in a way that nontechnical personnel can control them.

Managing a complicated legacy environment can be overwhelming.

I call the centralized process management tool the *BPM monitor*.

Until all systems have become message-oriented, transaction based, we must live with the legacy of decades of batch-oriented systems. The manager and business administrators understand the schedules and flow of the business better than the systems administrator or database administrator. Often these schedules are fluid and changing, and in many environments only technical personnel can make these changes. The BPM monitors where created for this group to use daily. The manager is freed from going through technical layers to control the systems they own.

Simplifying Administration and Control

The inability to centrally monitor the internal state of processes can be frustrating for administrators. This is especially true when managing large data processes. BPM monitors can be configured with messages in the process control view. The BPM monitor depicts every process in the system with an informative snapshot. Besides automatically scheduling processes, BPM controls processes that are queued or running—the manager can request an orderly stop to the process.

In IT convergence, business processes need not control every part of your system; it can be used on a pilot basis as a scheduling and logging tool for a subset of your processes. In fact, the BPM software can work 'out of the box' as an interface to the queue management facilities; however, this approach may not immediately help you improve the management of your environment.

Every complex application needs a master schedule that can manage all system processes. It should include all the controls needed to keep an application alive across the many processes. The master schedule of processes should be available to all the administrators for planning and management.

Natively, most legacy systems were not built with a simple high-level view of their schedules and status. There is no one-stop-shopping for the systems administrator to view the entirety of the processes that keep your application alive and well-fed. To do this requires surgery on the cryptic underbelly of the legacy system.

For instance, in an Oracle Database, administrators must query and format the data that hold job information to view the schedule in a useful form. Further, the Oracle Queue (DBMS_JOB) table only describes the most current queue, it only holds part of the critical information and it does not describe how the individual entries relate to each other. BPM improves control of these processes. After you have developed a schedule, you should be able to manually override the default process and reschedule for a warranting condition. With DBMS_JOB, you cannot see what a process is doing. To do this you must find the process identifier (PID) and query the DBMS_SQL views and then relate the results with the process and what it is doing—a complicated task.

The BPM method communicates process information with simplicity through small additions to your legacy procedures. To manage the system schedule you must be able to do four critical things: view the status, monitor what the process is doing, communicate with active processes, and view messages generated by the processes. Ad-hoc manipulation of a queue has to be done with cryptic (SQL*PLUS, CRON, AT) commands that your administrators might not be able to properly employ. All these actions are easily performed with the BPM monitor through a graphical, "point and click" interface.

BPM environments provide your managers and administrators with a master schedule that is independent of the features of the legacy systems. Business processes can be built for coordinated control. The processes will run uninterrupted until they are manually stopped. BPM and its simple development cycles create easily managed processes that can be gracefully shutdown and removed from a queue.

Controlling key data processes with CRONTAB scripts on UNIX servers, or the "at" command functionality of Windows-based servers, can be inefficient and frustrating. The BCP simplifies this by establishing a method to consolidate and centralize all processes into one application. The BCP allows administrators to schedule and coordinate individual process tasks at a proper timeline using its simple web-based interface. Moreover, the results of each process execution are viewable from the Internet.

Non-technical administrators have control over the schedule and frequency of execution of each process managed by BPM. They are not dependent on database and system administrators to change business and data processes. Also, it is simple to change the business processes to manage dependencies and coordinate control, including process suspension when two or more processes may interfere with each other.

A Process for BPM Control of Legacy Processes

Figure 6.1 displays a business process for moving legacy processes to control by BPM software.

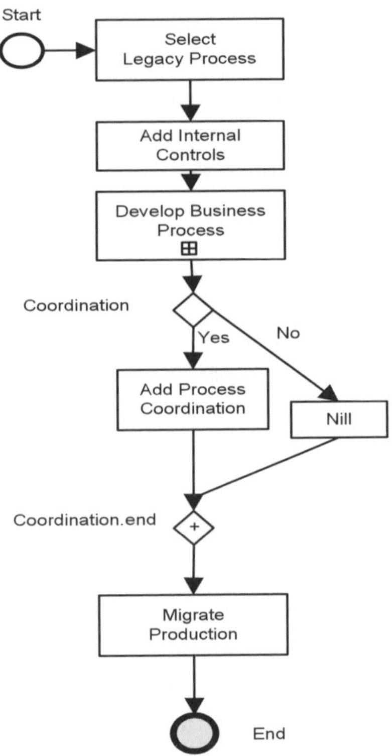

Figure 6.1 This business process shows the activities to migrate a legacy process into the business process environment.

For each of the legacy processes, the team retrofits it with limited controls. They add a small about of code to the process. I call the legacy procedure with limited controls a 'broker'.

Next, the team develops a business process that runs the broker. The process for doing this is the same as describe in chapter 3.

If the legacy process needs to be coordinated with other business processes, then the team adds this coordination into the business process diagram.

Finally, the team moves the business process into the production environment.

Concepts of Legacy Processes Under BPM Control

Figure 6.2 show a decomposition of the concepts of managing legacy processes with BPM software.

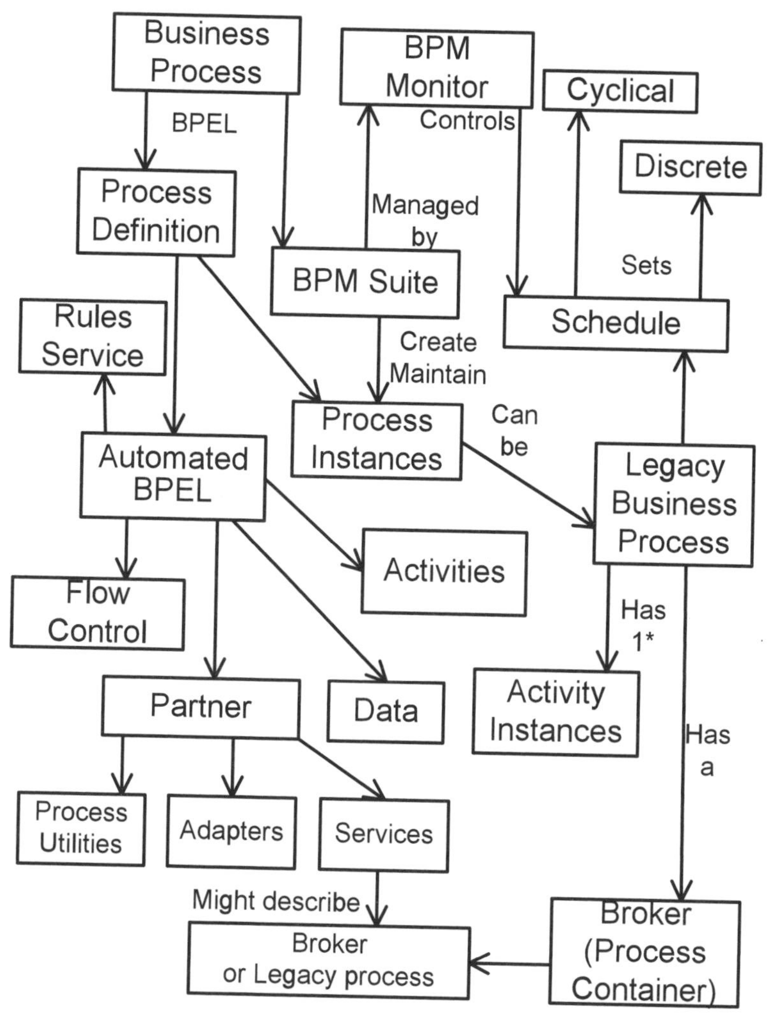

Figure 6.2 A concept decomposition of applying business process management techniques to the control of legacy processes.

A legacy business process controls a legacy system. If the IT Convergence team adds internal controls, logs and error conditions, then they are building a *broker*.

BPEL might define a broker as a service. BPM software can invoke many types of legacy processes through database middleware, COBOL gateways and other API's. If several processes need coordination, then your team can build business process that provide this coordination. Business processes can control a series of legacy processes or they can block other processes from running. The broker idea simplifies this.

Controlling legacy processes with BPM is simple. Managers can set and update the schedule of the process with the BPM monitor. IT schedules are either cyclical or discrete. A cyclical process is one that occurs on a regular time slice. A discrete process is a process that runs on exact calendar dates.

Process Management and Mismanagement

Everyone uses processes that feed operational systems, ERP and data warehouses. These might be scheduled or run manually. Global operations have forced the enterprise to be responsive over longer periods of time. The movement to web-centric applications has raised this need. Data processing in this new world has become more than a matter of reporting—it is a critical business function that organizations cannot afford to mismanage.

The approach I am describing uses business processes in the BPM suite to control and integrate legacy processes in your environment. The system process, hereafter called simply a process, is a repeatable, procedural task that must be performed regularly or semi-regularly. Every process has a beginning, an end, and an output and possibly an error status. There are 4 basic traits you should consider when controlling a legacy process with business process management:

- Every process must be started and stopped: sometimes stopped before it has finished its work.
- Every process should be monitored for performance.
- Every process should produce an activity log.
- Every process should produce a separate error log in case some exception or problem is met.

In more advanced control scenarios, processes can start other processes or block them from running or being queued. This is an ideal application of BPM diagrams (Chapter 3). BPM suites provide you with the tools to do this intricate management.

Your ideal system should function by breaking its objectives into some focused, discrete processes that are managed and monitored by the system administrator. In a BPM environment you let the owners of the processes service these processes themselves. You can group a series of related processes into a project and use the security provided by the BPM tools grant access to the managers.

If your application's processes are not separate and atomic, that is, many missions and objectives are done by a very few procedures, then you might wish to break these large programs down into many process with more focused objectives. Suggestions for doing this are discussed in this chapter. There is no limit to the size of the objectives of single processes with a business process, you can use the API to communicate with the web interface and see what the system is doing—breaking the process into focused parts will simplify the maintenance and operation.

Using BPM Tools to Control Processes

If some or all your processes are scripts that are started by CRON or by hand, then these might be wrapped into Java to be scheduled with BPM. Most BPM tools permit system calls; however, you will have less internal control with that approach. Each of the processes might be enhanced with the BPM's API or a common database table.

If you are changing key system procedures in a production environment, then this should only be done after a testing and cutover process.

In building processes into a manageable unit, we define a broker as an extension of the process concept:

- A broker is a legacy process, invoked and controlled by a business process that is managed by the BPM suite. The legacy process should be adapted for control by the BPM monitor and administered from a central location.

To build a broker that is managed by BPM suites, the process team should do two things. First, they wrap the legacy process in any language that is easy managed by the BPM suite. If the process is stored SQL, then it can be called with a JDBC connection. Second, create a business process that controls and communicates.

Suppose you have a legacy procedure that loads reference data from one database into anther database. Previously, the program was scheduled for execution with an 'at' command. The program is a stored procedure. To manage this with BPM software, all your process team need do is build a business process to execute the program. Figure 6.3 shows a simple business process for managing this.

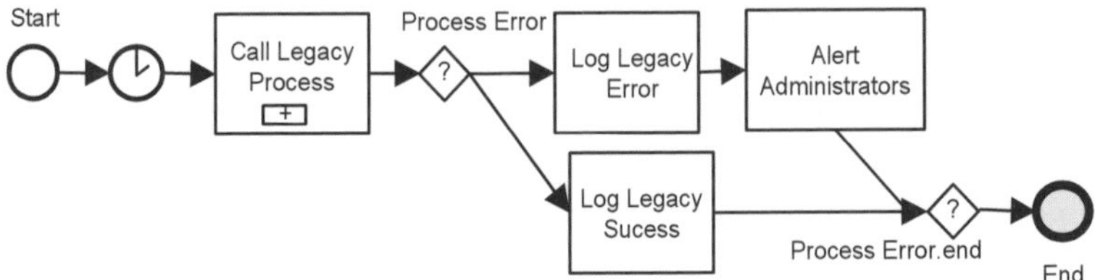

Figure 6.3 This business process diagram depicts a light-weigh, nondisruptive business process for integrating legacy systems. The legacy process is what I refer to as a broker. The clock denotes the schedule that is set by the BPM monitor.

This is the simplest method of using BPM software to manage a legacy process. Managers can change the schedule and view the history and status of the execution in this approach. I have found that most organizations require a bit more control than suggested in this diagram.

In more advanced scenarios, the broker can be scheduled, started or stopped, and communicates with its environment through the software API. The business process supervises calls to the process that has these capabilities. The broker's purpose is to lightly refactoring the process. With a broker process you only need to worry about the aim of the process, not how it is controlled by the administrator, or how it logs its success or failure. This control can be added with a few lines of code and should not intrude on the performance or the operation. Manipulating shared characteristics and behavior allows us to automate the management controls.

Typical Data Processes

Most processes arise from the need to move data from into the current system or out to another. Types of processes commonly encountered include:

Data feed loads. This includes the loading of reference data from legacy systems, FTP files from the internet, and transactions in various formats into your application system. Individual or closely related data sets should each have their own broker. Data feed loads are commonly read with Cobol, C, Oracle's stored file utilities or Java. Older processes might use older 3GL preprocessors. Most data loadings use common source directory for incoming files, and a location for archived files. With flat files, data loads open the source, perform data manipulation, and then move the file into an archive directory. Some data files have record counts at the header. Proper loading of these might call for every record be read to properly.

BPM tools approach this pattern in a flexible way, because these tools can use the arrival of a file to start the process. You activate the services when the files arrives, then move it to where the legacy program can read it. BPM services can read the contents of a directory, open every file with a certain extension, and other useful directory manipulation schemes. Most BPM tools fully implement FTP.

Data feed extracts. This is similar to a data load except that the output is a file. Often the extract involves opening SQL cursors against many tables. As with data loads the internal progress of the reporting or loading of a file can be difficult to trace without a monitoring tool.

ERP transactions. Operational data are reported to open interfaces and gateways to post. These processes can be more complex with the application of many rules, mappings, aggregations and segmentations of data. Often the ERP process is the most mission critical application program. If your system loads ERP transactions, then managing this with a business process can be the first step in converting it into a long running transaction.

Report generation. Time based reports are commonly scheduled processes. These scheduled processes produce a report in a specific format use formatting tools.

Notifications/messaging email notification. A key communications part of workflow is the transmission of email based on events and changes in the state of business activities. In the workflow, temporal business rules describe sequences of communications that are done.

Data warehouse publishing. Many organizations create their own extractions translation and loading processes to move data from an operational data store to the warehouse. These might involve many DML (data manipulation language) steps and cursors that aggregate the data for fact and dimension structures in the data warehouse.

As you consider these processes, you should see commonality with your system. If your processes are granular, then each one will do a named objective similar to the types shown here.

Current Practices

If your application is more than seven or eight years old, you probably see many layers of development artifacts in your environment. During the life of the application, developers have added many types of processes listed above. As technology developed, the practices for carrying out processes have changed.

Earlier practices use a combination of DML in scripts and database loading utilities. Shell scripts started the process with a simple scheduler such as CRON. These scripts exposed critical user names and passwords to the environment. Other variations of these early practices included running arcane tools such as SQL*FORMS in a batch mode.

More recent practices use Java stored procedures and PL/SQL procedures and middleware to do processing. This approach yielded more flexible and maintainable applications. The caution is that today systems are not scheduled with consistent tools. Some environments use a mix of CRON, AT and other utilities to manage their repetitious tasks.

The challenge is to merge older applications into a modern environment.

Motivations for Process Control

Enterprise systems work by breaking their tasks into many discrete processes that systems administrators oversee. Enterprise applications, those that feed operational systems, ERP and data warehouses, use these processes to carry out much of their mission. A monolithic database refreshes data through triggers, replication and stored procedures. But, there are many design requirements that motivate asynchronous movements of data. Coordinating these processes can be complex without a standard approach to process management. Business process management provides this standard.

Although a well formed, normalized database is the mandated norm for operational systems; your organization probably needs data from diverse external sources. Thus, your designers create applications whose critical reference data are provided by other business systems. For instance: mobile transactions might need validation after their posting. Critical data elements may arrive from other data sources, after transaction have been validated.

Enterprise integration systems (EIS) are often built to coordinate an application with the end-to-end business process that might not be present in other particular systems. One operation of the EIS is to add more business rules to the older system with the aim of lessening the manual steps that were involved in maintaining the system. For instance, two systems might have coexisted through manual entry of different, overlapping data elements. The EIS can end the manual entry by centralizing the reference data and transactions. The EIS carries out these interfaces through a series of processes that load reference data and validate and correct the harmonized transactions. The aim is to create system processes that coordinate asynchronous states of data and stop the manual fixes that previously maintained the two systems.

Because today's applications run in a diverse environment, processes must be coordinated across many systems, environments, and languages.

They use many types of data sources and outputs from XML, SQL*NET or flat files.

For all of these reasons, most organizations are motivated to manage their business processes. We have already covered the steps for developing a business process in Chapter 4. What I am suggesting is that business processes can manage the system processes that you have in your environment. This lightweight approach to BPM can move the organization more quickly into this technology, without rewriting the most detailed processes.

Legacy Process Control

Often, older processes were written with a naïve sense of their shelf life. For years, Developers have used Common UNIX methods on a server-by-server approach.

Besides the process tactics shown on figure 6.3, you should consider adding mechanisms for sending commands to your processes through messaging or programming strategies. With messaging you can build a flexible toolset for the control of the behavior and activity of a broker. BPM monitors provide you with job queues that manage and run a list of processes a specific timeline. With messaging you can control this job queue by assigning a state to the broker. Useful states include:

- GO: Allow the queue of this process
- KILL: Do not run this process, and stop it if it is already running
- ERROR: Do not run this process, an error occurred in the last run

Other processes can send the kill messages, or your team can design a simple web screen for this.

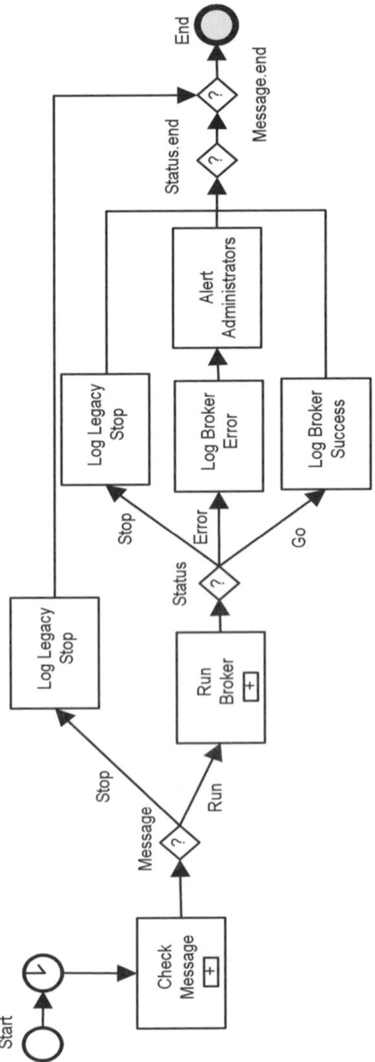

Figure 6.4 This business process diagram depicts a more robust way of integrating legacy systems processes.

Figure 6.4 shows a more flexible approach to managing legacy systems with Business Process software. To take this approach, your staff will need to add some code to the legacy programs. You can either develop a messaging strategy using the BPM's messaging API or you can create a simple data structure for communicating with the programs.

Looking at Figure 6.4, the process starts to perform its duties when it is first queued onto a job stack by the BPM monitor's timeline specification. The schedule queue is shown as a clock on the diagram. Once queued, the process starts to perform its tasks by calling the broker. During its execution, the broker can periodically poll a message queue for its control signals. You should add code to each broker to respond to the 'STOP' signal. The business process responds to the 'GO', and 'ERROR' messages. The 'GO' signal tells the BPM software to continue its normal management. The 'STOP' signal tells the broker to stop what it is doing as soon as it can, and return to control of the business process. The broker returns the 'ERROR' signal to the business process. If the legacy procedure encounters a severe error, it will signal an error condition to the BPM software. This occurs when the developer of the application has included an error message from the process.

For a process to respond to the 'KILL' or 'ERROR' signals, calls to the messaging API must be added to the broker.

Besides responding to messages, each broker can be setup to send messages and write logs to the text files (the "outside world") so administrators can quickly see what an active broker is doing or has done. The BPM monitor displays this messaging information and links it to the business process information.

When an active (queued) broker has finished its tasks, if it is set with a cyclical timeline it will automatically re-queue itself to run after time, otherwise it will run on the schedule or on demand. This strategy gives flexibility to administrators to create a schedule that meets complex needs.

For a broker to be "Active" (and therefore fully automated), it must satisfy two conditions. First, the BPM monitor must queue it. Second, it must have its state set to "GO". Under these conditions, the broker is performing tasks regularly and is considered "active."

For a broker to be "Inactive" (and therefore not scheduled to run), the manager should dequeued it or it is not blocked by another process.

To deactivate an "active" broker, an outside command would need to send a "STOP" message. When the control signal is set to "STOP", and the broker reaches its next polling point, it will see the "STOP" signal, stop its tasks, and return control to the Business Process. After all this has happened the broker will be in an inactive state.

There are two steps to activating an inactive broker. First, the state must be set back to "GO" by a message or command. If the administrator wishes to run the broker immediately, they start the process at the BPM monitor. When enabling an inactive broker, the administrator must ensure the control signal is set to "GO" before queuing the broker.

Broker Event Logging

The broker should log results of an individual run of the process including errors, notes about the start and end of the process and detailed debugging messages. To identify vexing issues that are difficult to reproduce in a development environment, you might use controlled debugging of the application in a test or production environment. Debugging messages might be put in the log or displayed using a separate part of the API. In either way, broker logs are viewable from the BPM monitoring and the BPM software can set the debugging level.

Email

BPM software provides detailed, active control to the administrator; however, some administrators might wish to have direct warning of issues and failures. Your team can add steps to the business processes to tell managers of selective process events. If a broker fails and is set to the ERROR status, you can add an email client to the business process client. Each member of the list assigned to the broker will get an email message. This allows pagers and cell phones to get messages. A business process can tell an administrator when its work is done or has failed for some reason. This cuts the on-site monitoring workload of the administrative staff.

Migrating Legacy Processes to BPM control

When the technical team in your organization is building a new operational system or meeting new requirements, they should use BPM techniques (Chapter 4).

You can combine new and old processes in the same enterprise view. The BPM approach develops processes that meet their immediate needs while coordinating their results with legacy processes. By using disciplined control process, you will achieve uniform error handling, process logging, and event posting. This combination will raise the productivity of your systems administration.

The project team should catalog each legacy process that must be managed and decide where it fits in the larger business processes. Categories of old processes should include loading data from external systems, workflow objectives, ERP transaction loading, and data warehouse population. By moving these into BPM control, you will start to understand their relationships.

Error Planning

When working with external systems, you will need robust, detailed error reporting to oversee the operational systems. You should develop error standards for each of the processes you migrate to BPM control. This includes when and where errors are reported and a process for tracking and recovery. With external interfaces, inconsistencies in design assumptions (file formats, maximum record counts), critical failures and errors occur from:

- Problems with database and operating system resources and
- Changes in external operational systems rules, file formats, transaction standards.

Moving your process control into the BPM environment centralizes standard error events. Systems administrator and managers receive immediate warnings.

Normal errors for a process might include changes in expected input, a lack of disk space for tablespaces, archived logs (or anything needing disk space) or archive copies of files, and exclusive locks on tables needed for insert. You can use messaging to raise error events. The message should state the error that occurred, when it occurred, and what program or operation, and the lines of code causing the exception. The report also might include data that caused the error.

Large Amorphous Packages

Lengthy programs that perform many objectives and wander across the requirements are commonplace; particularly those written over eight years ago. Factors that create this involve:

- The skill of the developers involved
- The use of anonymous blocks of code before stored packages
- Undisciplined corrections and additions

There are many advantages to breaking these into more discrete units.

- A process with one aim is simpler to understand and maintain. It is easier for a new developer to swallow smaller units of your application.
- A process with one aim is easier to debug.

Separating the process into more discrete steps needs a code walkthrough and manual reverse engineering of the functionality of the code.

If you work with large anonymous block of code you should wrap the block into a development environment that you can control. You can use debugging procedures to watch the application advance in a test environment. Combining messages with queries of the process results should clear up ambiguity in what the procedure is doing.

Look for parts of the code that carry out process steps in the large block. You might find redundant code that threads a process dependency in the single package.

At the conclusion of all these steps it should not be time-consuming to separate the procedure into more discrete steps.

Managing Legacy Processes With BPM

The BPM can control all the processes in the enterprise. BPM software logs broker queuing activities, monitors changes in process control and manages the job queue placement of the process based on the process schedule.

Broker Timeline

BPM monitors can control the timeline of most scheduled processes. The scheduled process runs on a timeline that is ether a fixed time between completions (cycle), or on a specific date and time (schedule).

A cycle or process cycle is the time between each execution. For instance, you might wish to start a process that polls for a database transaction or message every 5 minutes. Once the event occurs, it might take longer than the 5-minute cycle to process it. The business process does not start the program while the current process is running, so the execution time is not in the individual time cycle.

Examples of cycles include:

- Load transactions every 10 seconds
- Archive the transaction table every 2 hours
- Backup every 24 hours

In a schedule, the process starts at each date and time in a list. There might be several entries for the business process to run. Example schedules include:

- Produce sales report Monday at 10:00AM, Monday at 06:00PM, Friday at 10:00AM, and Friday at 06:00PM

- Replicate a large database schema on Friday at 11:45 pm, and on Wednesday at 00:15 am.

You will find the choice of using a cycle or a schedule is simple. If you are "polling" or "looping" for an event such as the arrival of a message or a change in the value in a table, then a broker should run as a cycle. Your managers can manually schedule a process that needs to run on at a specific time.

Legacy Process Dependencies

After you have connected the legacy process with a business process and the suggested internal controls, it is simple to set up dependencies with other legacy processes. A process might start another after successful completion, or yet another after meeting error conditions. Processes might also stop other processes from running and either re-queue them or leave them in a suspended state. To carry out these you build and deploy business processes with these capabilities.

One form of a dependency is process blocking. If there is a nearly continuous (or scheduled) process that must be stopped while another batch program is run, then build a business process that permits you to block that program while the other program is running. Figure 6.5 shows a fragment of a process, *Process A* that blocks another process, *Process B*, from running.

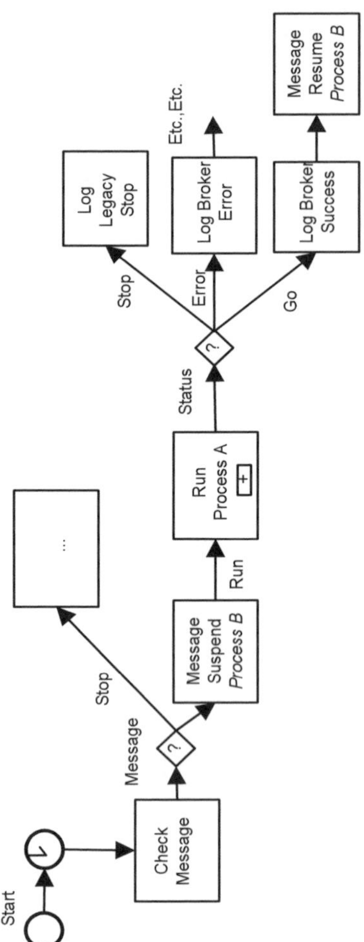

Figure 6.5 This business process fragment depicts a process suspending another process, performing its work then resuming the process \.

After it has been blocked, the process might either restart it, or it can be left off and wait for a manual restart by the administrator. The first scenario is used to prevent a transactions flowing into the system after a cutoff period. After the work is finished, the blocked process will be restarted. In another scenario, a process that was run because of a failure might block another process from running, thereby avoiding the corruption of a data and activities.

Summary

Using business process management to manage your legacy systems lets you continue to systems and systems interfaces while introducing standard controls. Through IT convergence, you can focus on a dramatic cut in complexity and application count. As your team develops with BPM, your organization can transition gradually, driven by business objectives, organizational patterns and projects.

Migrating legacy processes to "Brokers" and business processes improves control. The Business Processes yields five improvements:

1. Process control, the periodic, cyclical or on-demand control of processes,
2. Process prioritization, the starting or blocking of processes, depending on the outcome of events, you can put more than one legacy process in a business process diagram,
3. Log management including execution logging, debugging and error reporting,
4. System coordination and database administration, the control of the server's current resources assigned to the process queue, and
5. Performance management, the ability of the server to use current resources to perform data refresh and respond to process and user needs.

The BPM approach supports application administration by controlling (scheduling and frequency), prioritizing (blocking and chaining) and logging daily events that occur in the application and relaying selective results to the managers and administrators. Database and systems administrators work with resources and components of the architecture of the application to balance the user's needs with the performance requirements of the process queue. The aim is to keep the data current and coordinated in a previously confusing portfolio of applications.

The benefit of IT convergence is a greater understanding of your systems. The minds and unwritten practices of the personnel control this knowledge. By replacing legacy scripts and manual coordination with business processes, you can reorchestrate transactions and data flows to support the transition.

CHAPTER SEVEN

Technical Architecture

There are two chief design tools in the BPM/BR: business rules and business process management software. Each software package supports engines that run the rules and the processes. Because these engines use web services, they create a Service Oriented Architecture (SOA).

The SOA features late binding and web services; elements much needed by mobile computing. Mobile systems work with subsets of data in local databases. Mobile systems can still work when there is a discontinuity in network service, or where continuous service is not practical. For example, they can be onboard aircraft, ships or trucks. A business process approach can orchestrate transactions sent from mobile devices.

Challenges arise from today's enterprise integration problems. Businesses and government agencies aim to face these challenges with a composite application approach. A composite application can integrate multiple COTS packages, operational systems and external trading partners. However, with so many autonomous elements, there will invariably be overlapping terms and practices. The first benefit to the business is the enterprise unification of practices where the *best-of-breed* COTS systems are chosen to meet specific process needs. Business rules unifies the terms. So, the BPM/BR approach is an efficient way of building the composite application.

A composite approach with BPM/BR can move an organization from a legacy system to the new COTS. This is referred to as a *gating strategy*. With a gating strategy, large organizations can lower the cost and institutional shock of cutting out a legacy system. BPM/BR is particularity good at gating legacy ERP and the new ERP.

Business Process Management (BPM) runs composite applications with loose connection to business rule, databases, user interfaces and integration programs. Because it removes the dependences on the system running a process, maintaining the process is simple. It also simplifies the code changes by isolating changes in formats, process steps or system interfaces.

Business process management is important in two added areas: data warehousing and process administration.

There are three themes in the BPM/BR approach to the service oriented architecture:

- A business rules repository, connected to a business object server that positions rules for change, web services publishes the rule for processes to use,
- A business process engine and a process control capability that simplifies the control of business processes,
- An integrated business intelligence, ETL processes takes data from composite applications and populates a data warehouse

SOA places business practices where change will be simple. The architecture isolates the functions of the technical architecture that offer performance improvements and economic benefits. For instance the organization may wish to add a new COTS product, change a core process, or develop new business intelligence. By repeating these themes throughout the user interface, the process and the data warehouse, the architecture can achieve these objectives.

Business Object

In the first chapter I suggested the BPM/BR is an evolution of older methodologies. The BPM/BR architecture has been molded by the experiences of organizations that construct applications for the enterprise. These previous methodologies presumed a particular architecture. For instance Information Engineering created 'modules' based on functional 'CRUD' decomposition. Each module was directly connected to the databas with a proprietary language. The presentation layer is tightly bound or even a part of the business rules layer.

Figure 7.1 presents the older style of applications. The figure shows two forms of the same process, **Process x**.

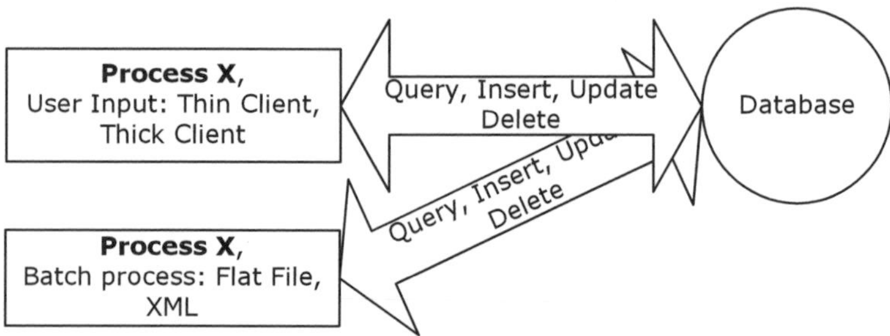

Figure 7.1 An example of earlier architectures with two different programs that implement the same process goal.

The top process runs with a screen and program code that query and update a database. This is the type of solution that might have been created by information engineering and CASE tools. The screen may be a thick client-server application with internal business rules and access to the database. Otherwise the applications may be a thin client web tier with the equivalent code in the ASP, JSP and HTML forms. The second box represents the same process, in a batch mode as implemented by loading a file such as an ASCII flat file or XML. The process could be a UNIX shell script, C program or something else. The point of the diagram is that this old style of writing programs was difficult to manage—it is hard to centralize your business rules when they are scattered among different processes. The programs may share development libraries however this does not eliminate the diffusion of business rules because there are multiple calls to the procedures in the two processes. Even the use of web technologies or XML does not solve the consistency issues—it merely recast it in a different technology.

There are additional issues with the simplistic architecture show with Figure 7.1:

- Scaling issues, having multiple clients or session interacting directly, with no data caching, with the database can lead to contention.
- Proprietary languages, the use of this architecture, might put the business rules in a scripting language such as PowerBuilder™, Delphi™, and other tools. Even web development tools such as Cold Fusion™ have their own languages.
- Inflexible architecture, any change to the database requires a

change to the application. Any changes to the application require changes to the business process(es) that it participates in.

- Poor security model, the security of the application is dependent on a system that may not be directly connected to the process. For instance, security may be an attribute of the database server.

This was a fragile way to develop applications—changes in the requirements can inflict violence to the production code.

Isolating the Business Rules

Figure 7.2 shows a more robust approach to developing solutions. In this architecture the two processes communicate with a common business object through a common set of messages. The business object performs all of the business rules validation and controls the access to the database. Actions performed by the business object are governed by the security certification of the calling client.

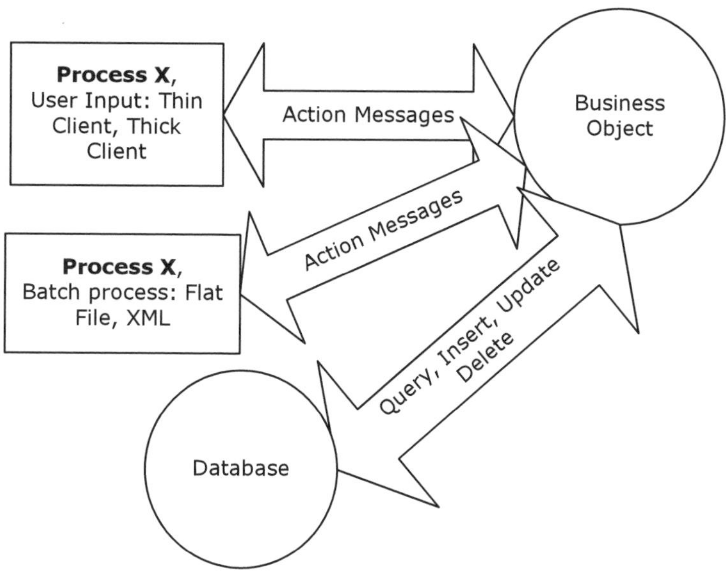

Figure 7.2 A architectural solution to a batch and user process as implemented using a shared business object and a message structure.

Figure 7.2 displays an early version of the loosely connected architecture.

The business rules are positioned for change because they reside in the business object on the server. In object oriented parlance, a business object is a business use case. Traditionally, business objects interact with data objects. Figure 7.2 shows the data objects residing in the database.

Because the business object could be generated (not executed) by the business rules repository (BRR), they originate from a centralized source. A policy that might affect many business objects can be propagated by a change in the BRR. Finally, this approach truly supports collaboration and reuse.

The business object approach shown in figure 7.2 is better in these ways:

- Better performance: the business object strategy can use threads and caches,
- Improved, yet inflexible architecture, most business objects strategies use code, not engines to run the business rules,
- Improved security: because no user access to the database is needed and the business object can be placed in application servers,

The approach is less fragile than the simplistic approach of the past. Changes to database schema need changes to data access objects. Business rules are isolated at a single point.

The decoupling of the application from direct interaction with the persistence layer has been around for many years. The architectural approach in Figure 7.2 is further modernized by a business process management approach. In the BPM/BR approach, the business rules in our use case use activities that are a part of a composite application.

Isolating the Process

BPM/BR strives for the architecture shown in Figure 3.3. The business object is decoupled from the batch or user interface in the process by the business process execution language (BPEL) server. Indeed the database is entirely absent. This is important because technologists believe that the database will play a declining role in the future. Someday, BPM software will hold all business data in the flow of the process.

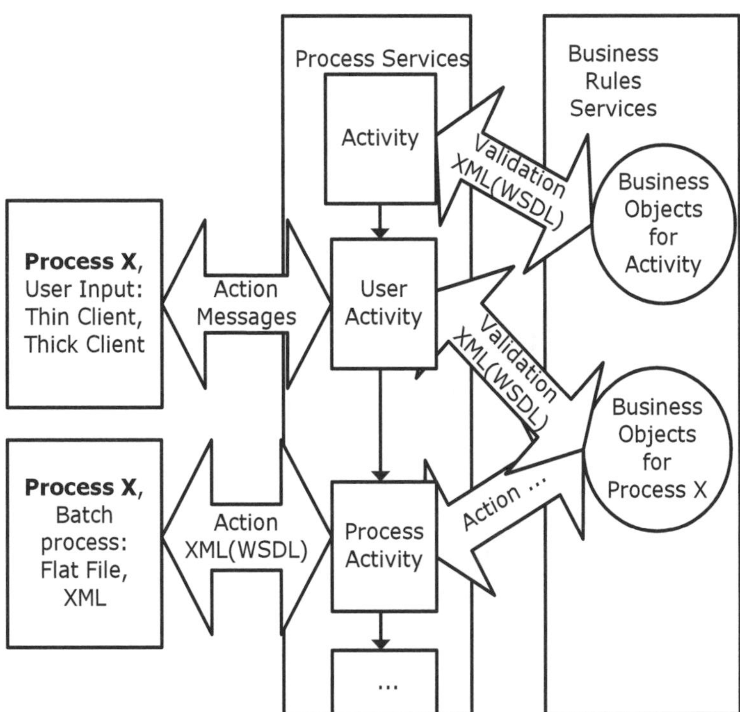

Figure 7.3 This is architecture with using a shared business object and a BPEL server.

The benefits of the architecture in figure 7.3 are:

- Services can be loosely connected through web services or messaging
- Agile Architecture, since processes and rules are run by an engine, not coded or generated, they can reflect rapid change
- Rapid Changes for Business

Figure 7.4 shows a business process design that implements these ideas. This shows how the file loading process and the user interface share the same infrastructure. This includes a connection of the application to the ERP.

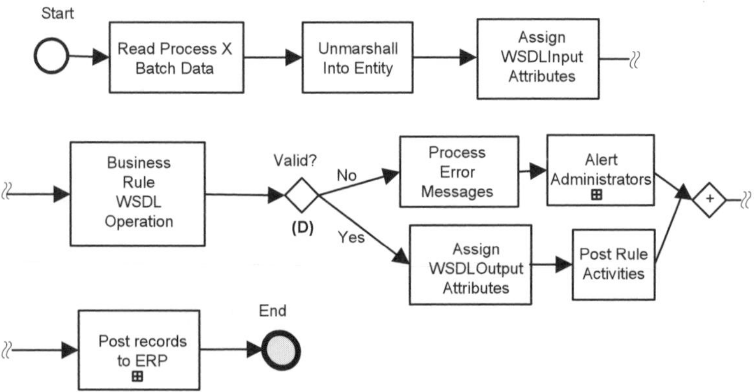

Figure 7.4 An business process modeling (BPM) diagram for to a batch and user process as implemented using a shared business object as part of a larger business process. The final step of the process is a posting of the transaction to the ERP.

Figure 1, 2 and 3 mark the evolution of the application architectures over the last decade. The process activity shown on figure 7.4 is a part of a larger process.

Integrating the Enterprise IT Ecosystem

Today's enterprise architecture is a collage of operational systems, COTS, legacy systems and data warehouses. With previous practices, such as screens placing records in a database (Figure 7.1), IT organizations integrated these with fragile solutions. The IT 'ecosystem' has been built up with relational data modeling, OOSE, client server, web, data warehousing, and various types of ERP and COTS products. The result is an infrastructure with a milieu of disjointed programs.

To grasp the BPM/BR architectural concepts, it is important to comprehend why this new approach is needed. Architectures such as shown in Figures 7.3 and 7.4 reduce this complexity. The aim is to change the way the application is integrated, updated and managed. The application should be loosely connected to other parts of the enterprise system (Figure 7.3) and everything should be a part of a larger business process.

Application integration is one of the top challenges facing business and IT organizations. The broad integration objectives of the enterprise should be supported by strategic modeling and process management activities. These objectives are the starting activities of the BPM/BR. Much of the evolutions of the early analysis are the outcome of different peoples experience with developing, deploying then supporting eBusiness and application integration architectures.

Challenges of Integration

For many large enterprises, integration is a top spending expense. The complexity and scope of information technology drive high costs of integration. Organizations have been assembling standards and practices to simplify the challenges of integration. Software vendors are motivated to adopt these standards.

Business Rules and Business Process Management are part of these standards and practices. They are the foundations of BPM/BR. The organizations include the Business Process Management Organization (www.bpm.org), the business rules form (www.businessrulesforum.org) and the business rules special interest organization in the Object Management Organization (www.omg.org).

IT integration is a response to competitive pressures and globalization of business. To participate, companies, organizations and governments must become more integrated and connected with their partners and customers.

Prevailing economic conditions motivate businesses to improve efficiencies in all operations including IT. These economics call for companies to cut product-cycle times, time- to-market; and to attend to their company's management needs. Mergers, takeovers, divestitures, and changes in regulations complicate integration measures. Today, companies have a raising need to tie together their disparate systems in an unprecedented way.

To contain integration cost, enterprises must replace or reuse legacy systems and stove-piped operational systems. Yet, programmers never intended for legacy systems to be integrated. They never provided open interfaces or application program interfaces. To replace or combine systems, organizations have integrated or retrofitted their old systems with COTS technologies. These include Business to Business, supply chain (SCM) integration solutions and customer-relationship-management solutions (CRM).

In the software industry, there are many enterprise application integration (EAI) technologies, including offering from Tibco, WebMethods, SeeBeyond and other companies. Some application servers such as BEA's WebLogic and IBM's WebSphere have EAI capabilities. Financial services, insurance, health care, telecommunications and marketing have been early adapters of these.

Often, the enterprise runs on various systems. Over decades, these have grown on different platforms using different technologies. IT groups built systems for specific business and technical reasons and often for small divisions or departments. Legacy systems are frequently 'stovepipes'—they are disconnected and fulfill meager purposes.

Other technologies in the IT portfolio can be COTS. Sometimes new COTS packages and legacy systems have redundant capabilities. A massive investment in Y2K remediation gave many legacy systems new life. Legacy systems are on different platforms using different architectures including: Cobol IDMS, client-server, web-based applications, batch, and real-time synchronous applications. Despite Oracle and DB2's marketplace dominance, applications use different databases. Depending on the age and type, designers designed each data model differently. The result is a wide array of different transactional and process control systems. Each system has different data-entry styles, from the Web to batch mode.

From this it is easy to see how the complexity of integration grows with the size and the age of the enterprise. In the United States Department of Defense (DoD), the Defense Finance and Accounting System (DFAS) is responsible for the accounting. DFAS estimates that they have over 400 legacy systems. This is the result of information technology that spans 40 years.

Besides architectural differences, integrations affect many layers of changing technology. XML and webs services are replacing Corba and EDI. Vendor specific middleware becomes antiquated with time. Styles of web development have developed and bifurcated into many different approaches. Java Server Pages replace Microsoft's active server pages (ASP). The Java/JSP techniques can be even further refined with 'open frameworks'. For instance the Struts project abstracts the presentation layer from the business rules.

Because it is a self-describing and standard-message format, XML has solved some of the semantic problems of EAI. But standard schemas in XML have changed slowly. In one industry the enterprise may have to deal with multiple schemas. Yet, EAI needs to develop and provide transformation and translation between XML messages and between systems.

Even the when they have built the enterprise from software from one vendor, IT organizations need EAI. In a single vendor solution, one 'universal' ERP manages all business processes. Despite available universal applications, a purportedly complete IT infrastructure, there is a set of secondary applications surrounding the ERP.—Quality, Maintenance Management, Inventory Control, Regulatory automation.

Most large corporations run with various ERP applications including SAP, Oracle Financial or JD Edwards, SCM including i2, Manugistics, Human Resources with PeopleSoft, CRM with Siebel. Figure 7.5 shows some of secondary software that feeds the ERP. It includes fleet management, maintenance management, real estate and various quality analytical or engineering tools. Some of these systems might be COTS. IT organization might be responsible for some applications. Many of the stovepipe's capabilities are contained in the enterprise's COTS packages.

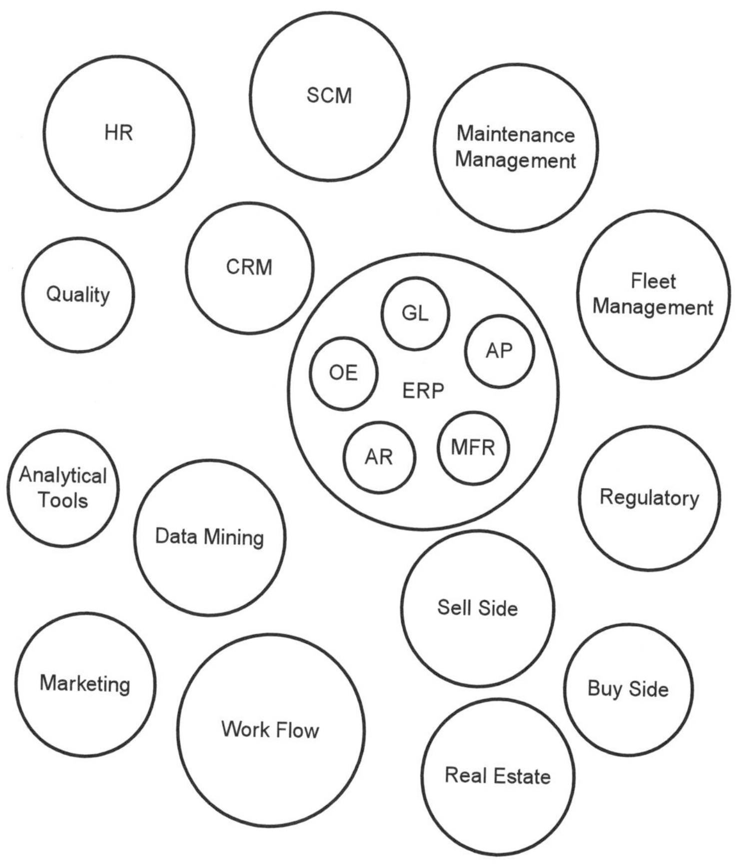

Figure 7.5 A high level component diagram of today's enterprise ecosphere is a constellation of various applications.

For instance, imagine Figure 7.5 describes an enterprise application ecosystem. Each application needs many combinations of overlapping entities. A small set is:

- Human resources is the source for personnel, the ERP, Supply Chain Management (SCM), customer relations management (CRM), maintenance management, and real estate need these data

- The ERP is the source for orders and customers, the CRM, SCM, Sell Side, and marketing applications need these data
- The ERP is the source of fixed assets, the maintenance management, real estate, and fleet maintenance application need these data

There are many more data needs. As the source system changes the data entity, the interface must report the change to the data consumers. To report these changes, the interface must transform attributes. In a point-to-point interface strategy, each application uses a different interface with different protocols.

There is a need to share information outside the enterprise. Each IT organization needs complex EAI across this hodgepodge of systems that organizations have installed over the years.

On the buy side, companies have systems like Agile, Arriba, CommerceOne. On the sell side they might have Seybold, Clarify, Onyx, or Broad Vision. These systems have been built with different methods and with specific needs in mind. Organization need to integrate these disparate systems.

Semantic integration unifies the transaction's meaning and context. Enterprises add special policies and procedures with a business rules approach. They can develop process flexibility with Business Process Management (BPM). At the highest maturity level, process control creates autonomous processes including mobile processes. Changing standards for BPM include the ability to publish and exchange business processes.

Clearly integration is not an easy feat. BPM/BR techniques simplify integration problem domains in an IT ecosystem. BPM/BR uses a combination of the best practices that works with the technical architecture.

Historical Methods of Integration (Integration Through Retrofit)

In today's environment, there are two main approaches to integration. The older method is a custom Point-to-Point Integration. I call this style of integration the retrofit. A retrofit occurs when programmers quickly insert the interface and heroically bolt it onto the architecture. The next approach is a business process approach that is integrated along a communicating backbone.

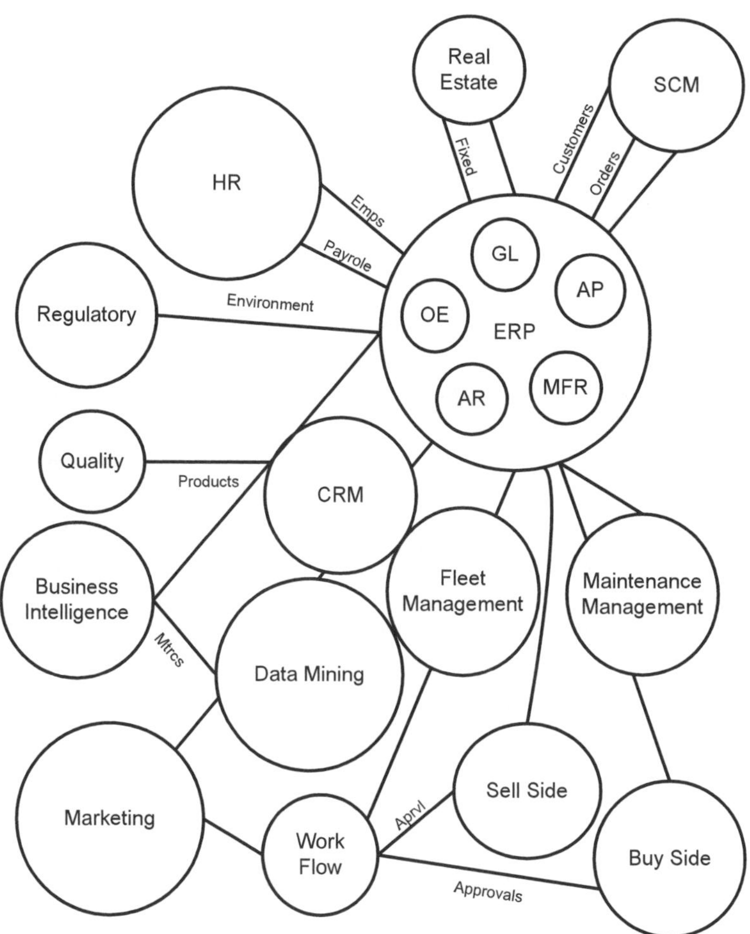

Figure 7.6 A point-to-point approach is developed with a narrow focus on the integration needs of the organization.

In a point-to-point integration, programmers retrofit each application with nonstandard custom business rules and processes. Next, they write programs for applications, data consumers that share data with the integration. This approach is costly and rigid to create and maintain. Without a centralized server the integrations:

- Apply the same business rules in different application and languages
- Perform processes using different reporting or logging standards and methods

- Control the processes with different scheduling and coordination strategies

Also, every year the enterprise adds new technologies. New systems need connections to other systems. When the IT team adds business intelligence to these new systems, they retrofit the data with ETL modules. When anything changes—data, business rules or processes—the IT team changes every affected application.

Point-to-point integration projects narrowly address an aim. They create integration points that are fragile or unbending. Over the long run, they are more expensive to change. The point-to-point approach is redundant and inefficient. In summary, this is a costly, time-consuming and invasive approach. Point-to-point integrations can be a large part of the enterprises IT budget.

Taking the strategic approach, one that is more configurable, calls for an early investment. Yet, as processes and business rules change, the investment will pay off. Each business process might involve procedures and transactions across some systems. In the BPM/BR managers direct the integration systems overtime as part of a centralized decision-making process. The IT teams carry out the interfaces one-by-one and design them to fit into the long-term plan. In a 2002 study, the Gartner Group reported that organizations experienced a large IT cost cut using a strong business rules approach. The key to using the BPM/BR is to plan strategically; companies should develop a long-range plan for loosening the connections between applications. Next, they tactically develop the first of a series of integration using a BPM/BR approach.

The Role of the Operational System

All organizations, even those that extensively use commercial software, develop some custom applications. For instance an enterprise might create a special web-based application for an ERP's order entry module. I call this an operational system. Increasingly, operational systems handle the integration needs of the enterprise. Software vendors and open source products provide sophisticated, comprehensive solutions to business problems. Operational systems tend to focus on the branded product line and customer services of the business.

In the federal government, organizations are mandated by the Clinger-Cohen act to secure commercial products and integrate their practices with these products. The operational system's nature is changing. The web screen connected directly to the database is less likely to be written; the enterprise is devoting its resources on core integration and business rules efforts.

Why the Composite Application is a More Strategic Approach to Integration

BPM/BR loosely couples programs to the architecture. Web services interact among presentation layers, integration processes, extraction and translation processes and BI applications. The BPM or business rules define the protocol for every layer or application. The result is comprehensive interface specifications for processes and business rules. These specifications tell how to communicate with all the applications.

One long-term aim of this approach is to standardize every application's business rules so IT teams can reuse them across other integrations. So everyone should know where rules are and how they are used. In the enterprise, a developer should be able to explore a server(s) web services directory to find out how to use a business rule set.

Centralized business rules cut the cost and improve the flexibility in connecting all the applications. The enterprise can lower costs by selecting open source technologies or using a competitive practice in a COTS package. Through the business rules services, they then add their 'cultural fingerprint' to rules by feeding transactions and integrations to the COTS packages.

All BPM/BR activities are managed in the business rules/process repository. In the rules repository, there are reusable components, including:

- The way data formats are defined,
- The 'signatures' of business object, the way it is used,
- The data mapping tools and functional tools.

The business rules repository simplifies building interfaces to other applications by creating common business objects. Delivering the business object from the BRR is just one advantage of the strategy. More improvement for integration with the BPM/BR includes:

- Applications running in BPM software might use real-time and batch integration. Teams can convert a point-to-point solution, which only supported batch mode, into one with real-time characteristics.
- The environment can change rapidly.
- The BRR creates mappings that connect to enterprises outside the organization for B-to-B and SCM integration as well.

BPM creates real-time visibility and asynchronous control of multistep business processes. Businesses that do this easily adapt to new applications and organizational changes.

Integration With Trading Partner's Systems

BPM/BR is not limited to internal systems. Its powers combine customer and trading partner applications and processes. For instance, the IT team uses BPM techniques to share processes with trading partners. BPEL is designed for this.

WDSL and BPEL are standards that simplify this exchange of process information with trading partners and customers. BPEL connects transaction validations against business rules through published WSDLs.

BPM develops a system without point-to-point integrations. The BPM/BR architecture creates application at a lower development cost with higher manageability of integrations requirements. BPM incorporates the specifics of the operating systems, security issues and the standards involved and the technologies. It supplements the scope by refactoring legacy systems. Each project contributes to a centralized business rules server.

Figure 7.8 presents an abstract outline of a BPM/BR approach to EAI. The figure shows three layers of application integration—enabling one application to talk to another. The core components enable:

- Connection into the applications, when it is through a WDSL there is a 'w' inside a circle
- Validation of the transaction against a business object that is always published as a WSDL
- Transformation of passing message attributes, or a change of the message into the form understandable by the application, as denoted by subscripts
- Control and management of the data flowing between applications.

These are parts of the BPM/BR architecture. General design considerations include:

- The way the services are invoked
- Supporting technologies
- The sequencing of the actions.

Often, legacy systems support batch processes. Your team might design a messaging scheme through a process that spoofs the transaction.

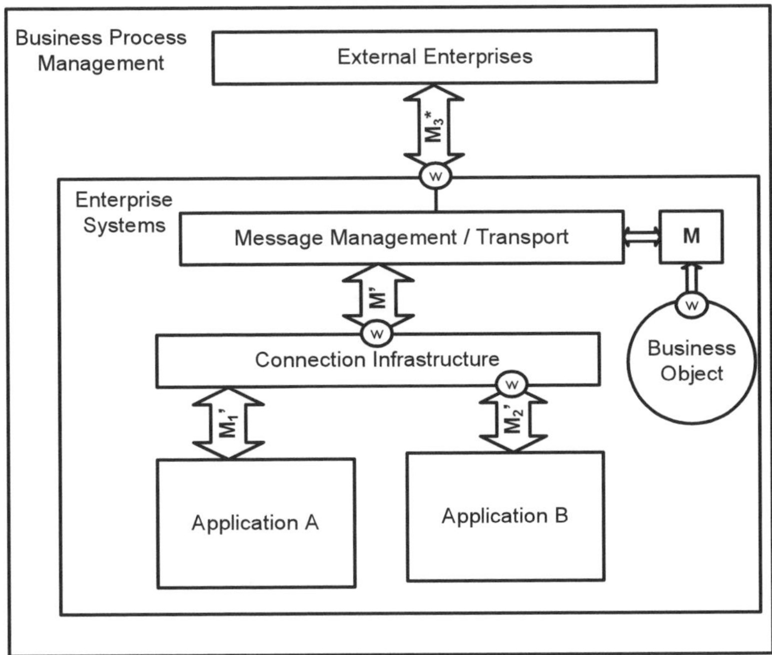

Figure 7.7 The powers of the BPM/BR platform support a web services and messaging.

One layer of Figure 7.7 is the Business-to-Business Integration. This layer connects to external enterprises using their security and protocols and enveloping. The two applications act as a composite. The message **M** is a request for some operation in the two applications. The process translates the message and directs it to the correct internal application and external applications, as in a B to B scenario. The business object processes the rules. The message is bidirectional in this example. The transport layers translate the message into a form that can be consumed by the applications. Business process management controls the nature, timing and the message flows.

In a composite application approach, business process management integrates many participants including different systems and users. Managers use BPM software to oversee these processes as they run. To implement this, each application needs an adapter component loosely shown as the bidirectional arrows. The adapters are responsible for communicating the proper style and content.

Integration Messaging

A messaging approach to integration is needed to build a loosely connected infrastructure in a few situations:

- Mobile processes that are not a part of the enterprise network
- Interfaces to complex, composite applications where web services would be inefficient.

To integrate and control, the communications infrastructure or middleware is responsible for sending messages to systems. As shown in Figure 7.8, there are the four major communication patterns between systems in a message transportation system.

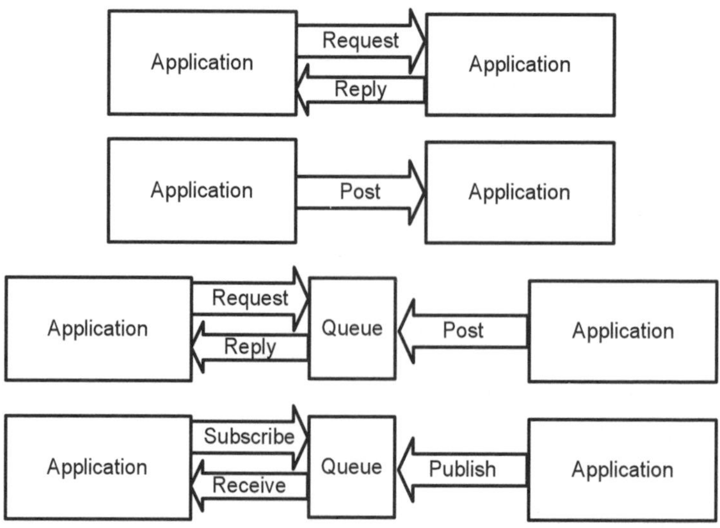

Figure 7.8 There are four styles of message-passing in EAI scenarios.

The first pattern is request/reply. This is similar to use of a terminal/database application. From a systems perspective, a process sends a request and then suspends processing until it gets a response back. This is a synchronous or time-sensitive process where systems, such as within a data processing environment, must be online while it passes the message.

The next pattern is simple message passing. An external system sends a document, such as an EBXML request for an order of products. Next, it gets a confirmation of the request. Unless an error occurs, there is no more business information returned. Just as in the first style, this is a direct system-to-system communication, and the synchronous, direct message passing requires that systems be online.

The next two patterns use messaging queues to support an asynchronous form of messaging. The queues serve as staging locations between systems. With simple messaging and queuing a message can move from application to application with certainty, even when the target system is not online.

A more advanced technique is to employ publish-and-subscribe messaging. This assumes a loose coupling among the systems involved. This technique is implemented in Sun's JMS and in Microsoft's .Net. It is similar to an email client such as Outlook. For instance, an application publishes a message object to a queue, such as a shipment notice, and it need not know the details of the final recipients of the message object. Receivers register themselves as subscribers that pull the messages from the queue. The advantages to this are the few dependencies between the publisher and subscriber. Applications, for various reasons, can dynamically add or remove subscribers. So if the new system is updated with shipment notices, they subscribe to the messages.

Broadcast and subscribe is increasingly being used to loosely couple systems. The messages need to be translated and harmonized among the different needs. This core capability is provided by business rules engine. It transforms and formats the message. Process management routs the data.

Business Rules in Message Translation

The business rules activity defines what a business does and processes define how it integrates this into the architecture.

Often, applications and the processes that monitor and control them have different data structures and application interfaces. Messages pass from application to application in several different ways. The business rules architecture transforms the messages and applies rules. The business activities process the business rules and transform the data from a central source. The first translation is syntactic. This is a reformatting, parameter by parameter, of the message into a form acceptable by the target system. Transformation can be as simple as a date change, or it might certify each of the supplied parameters is in the proper format.

Business processes intelligently route data among systems. When a sequence of business activities runs, the system interprets its contents and then orchestrates related systems. Business rules transformations meet the semantic needs of the process. Based on the meaning of the data, semantic rules alter the data, apply constants and derive attributes. Rules perform other translations. For example, a rule might translate an attribute from a local standard to an industry standard.

The business rules repository holds a common intermediary and independent format between the applications and systems. This is known as a canonical format. You use the canonical format to cutout point-to-point interfaces. Canonical rules translate the message from X to Y, which is the canonical intermediate format, and then on from X to Z. The point-to-point design converts a message from X to Z. Canonicals decouple the format of the messages passing between the systems. This is similar to the messaging queues that decouple the message transport. With canonicals, a change to System X should not cause a change to the other data consuming systems—it is isolated by this intermediate message format. The purpose of this modeling technique is to create layers of abstraction that isolate changes in systems.

Users of COTS software configure data to meet enterprises data needs. These are known as 'flexfields' in Oracle financials. For instance, many organizations use SAP's physical plant module to perform fleet maintenance. The SAP application is configured with the fields needed to turn the generic equipment into a vehicle. With this flexibility an organization configures the COTS to display their own fields and carry out customized business practices. What is missing from these fields is a way of validating and translating the fields with business rules. Business rules can manage these data. Through interfaces an enterprise can add its own business rules to these configurable fields and reflect their needs in the application.

Data warehouses need to subscribe to the business information in the messages. By using a messaging backbone, a process can catch and perform extraction translation and loading of the information in the systems.

A Unified Interface

Ideally, the SOA (BPM/BR) carries out processes in one interface, exposed as a web service on the internet. As needs arise, such as creating a new product offering on the web, IT teams easily design new systems with centralized business rules and processes

We have discussed message transport and transformation. The next topic is the interfaces into the applications. There are several common interfaces:

- Batch mechanisms, such as an FTP file transfer
- Transactions or real-time requests through HTTP or direct TCPIP communication.

Like the core process I discussed in chapter 3, Interfaces should be language and platform independent. This is the reason the service oriented architecture is so important. Combining WDSL and BPEL can enable:

- Unified interface that handles the application connectivity
- Data transformation
- Intelligent routing for the transactions and messages passing between systems.

With SOA each intermediary and adapter communicates with other applications. Where needed, message queues perform the work. The work can be putting in orders, updating records, and others.

Integration with the SOA hides complexities of different operating environments —communications, protocols. This is the advantage of using a framework based on WSDL and BPML. Integrating systems with ERP is similar to integration into a legacy COBOL system that looks similar to some other integration.

As companies try to compete and outmaneuver each other for market leadership, management of the supply chain is increasingly important. Business-to-business integration has become essential. In a BPM/BR approach these systems can act like sending and receiving mail. The communication with an external entity needs partner management. In one scenario imagine a parent organization with many divisions. The system must send many transactions in many protocols. The system would need to manage the protocols. It sends and receives EDI, or Rosetta Net, or Biztalk messages back and forth. The adapters have to manage message authentication to ensure it is directed to the correct destination. Message encryption and decryption protects the message contents moving across the public internet. With transaction message nonrepudiation all parties agree on what was sent and received.

For example, a customer sends an order. The B-to-B component de-envelopes it. Based on the protocol that was used, the process authenticates that it came from a partner. It decrypts the contents. Business rules validate it for formatting according to the protocol. More rules apply to the transactions in that message. Process management moves them to the correct application. Finally, the process returns an acknowledgment response to that customer. Everyone knows that everything was successfully processed.

One of biggest challenges of B-to-B is the high cost of adding trading partners. For instance, with EDI, 80 percent of suppliers historically have been unable to use EDI because of this cost. The methods, different technologies or lack of infrastructure in place has prevented them from supporting an expensive EDI system. For businesses entering the new world of XML and B-to-B, rapid adoption of these technologies establishes liquidity in market-places. BPM/BR yields rapid on-ramping of small-to-medium enterprises.

The Process Integrated Development Environment

The previous section talked about how organizations used to develop integration and the ideal they are striving for now. I am going to tell you how the BPM/BR is a method for building the environment you need. In the last sections I inferred that:

- Point-to-point integrations are a fragile way of developing applications
- Tight bindings to the database is one point-to-point integration technique
- A messaging, EAI architecture offers an environment that hosts loosely coupled activities in the business process environment

The BPM/BR addresses many the challenges in building an EAI architecture. There are 5 components to the BRR integrated application environment (IDE):

- The business rules repository (BRR) that consists of the Business rules workbench, the metadata repository, business rules engine
- A process server that runs the BPEL processes the BPM team created. The process server might host the ETL processes for the data warehouse
- A data warehouse server that hosts the star schema as populated by the ETL processes in the process server
- A process management server that monitors, schedules and coordinates legacy processes in the process server.

These components align business and the IT infrastructure because:

- They place business rules in one place so it is easy to change how an organization works
- New user applications, processes and data warehouses can be

quickly created updated or removed

- The processes can become a part of a business processes management strategy
- Interfaces to other systems as trading partners are simple to change

These architectural components are the outcome of the activities of the BPM/BR.

Business Process Management

Business Process Management is the outer layer of Figure 7. BPM manages information flows across the integrated systems. It works at a higher business level to simplify management control. Business managers and systems administrators control the processes. A business rule surgically adapts the data validation and transformations in information flows. Processes occur before rules. So an early activity of the BPM/BR is modeling the business process using BPML activity diagrams. Business process modeling:

- Unifies the business owners of the process and the technical implementers
- Enables the collaboration with systems needed for the composite application to work
- Identifies where and how business rules are to be introduced and enforced
- Standardizes how the exceptions and alternate processes are to be managed.

Each activity in the process either requests the services of a partner or it collects input from an end user. The end user can be an employee, customer or partner. This may happen in a workflow scenario. As the process runs, each activity does the assigned task based on the business logic. When the process runs in a monitoring environment; the managers see an aggregated view of all data. This is independent of the differences in the systems.

A benefit of this approach will reduce needs for database services. As the process team configures long running transactions in the business process software, they also configure the data (persistent storage). Business process query language (BPQL) gets to these data elements. For example, a BPM creates one view of all the orders in a composite application. This is independent of the inventory systems or order-management systems. The BPM team creates a single view of the business forms in the process diagram. Traditional data modeling is unnecessary. Therefore, the need for data modeling and database management will become a systems administration chore.

BPM manages exceptions in the business rules validation and the process. The BPM team can build processes that remove long-running transactions. This removal might involve a dozen different systems. This is referred to as the compensation part of the process model.

BPM manages all the data available in the process. This includes the data 'between' the activities. An ETL process can provide this timing data to business intelligence analysis. For example, an analysis could identify inefficiency in a business rule for an interface to a legacy system. With a revision to the business rules or to the processes, the enterprise can add logic into the rules to filter those out and trap the inconsistencies, and increase performance.

Mobile Processes and Business to Business Processes

Global IP communications is becoming increasingly common. Different technologies are spreading wireless IP networks. For instance, WiMAX (Worldwide Interoperability for Microwave Access, IEEE 802.16e) is set to become the "next big thing" in the mobile technology world. WiMAX implements a Metropolitan Area Network. WiMAX allows users to connect to the internet at broadband speeds while being many miles away from, and out of line-of-sight of the transmitter. A less rich mobile technology is WAP (Wireless Application Protocol). WAP has become the standard for wireless "terminals" such as smart phones. Where do these technologies fit in with the three themes we have been discussing throughout?

As bandwidth spreads, the customer and trading partner act as virtually connected components in the composite application. Someday, the business process will support application on mobile computers. Processes will spread economic information into the user's pocket—even when the application runs on a plane, automobile or ship. This advance will need to process many complex transactions.

Mobile applications present many challenges. For instance, mobile applications should not reveal sensitive or irrelevant information. For the mobile application:

- If it is a trading partner then they should only see their orders or contracts,

- If it is a customer then they should only see their own data,
- If it is a local distribution point then they should only see their own customers and inventory information.

Data security is only part of the issue. We want to be able to develop an application that we can drop onto the mobile device as easily as we send a document.

The mobile enterprise will be able to interact with the composite application. Some of the benefits will be:

- In-transit inventory becomes visible: where it is and in what quantities,
- Complex sensors can be deployed and scanned for input,
- Customer is continuously available—offering and orders are quickly routed to the customer and trading partner,
- If business rules can be pushed then changes in policies and procedures will be simpler to maintain,
- The task of knowledge management will be reduced

These are some of the benefits of application is a mobile environment. Even with a globally perfect communications network connectivity is not widespread. This architecture will need a new technology: agent technology. In theory, agents can post transactions, pass documents or information request without the benefit of continuous communications.

To play a role in the composite application, autonomous enterprise agents (AEA) need business rules, reference data and validation services. These agents communicate with other agents. The AEA might fail gracefully and arbitrate corrections for the user.

Because the connection is not always available, the agent or application must queue the transactions, prepare the queue for consumption and arbitrate the failure of a transaction for correction. Systems correct the data at the enterprise or at the source. The AEA will need to

- Set up and arbitrate a service request,
- Validate the transaction,
- Move documents to the enterprise.

AEA can refresh the local application. The agent AEA might use the services of the BPEL engine to interact with the enterprise. One activity might gather reference data for the AEA. It builds a queue and publishes data to the relevant subscribers. Services in this environment keep track of whom gets that data, how long they need to see it and when they get it. The business process coordinates with the rules engine to get the correct data into the reference data queue.

The native powers of the BPEL server can service the mobile process. Activities in the process can classify the types of replication that are needed to manage the rules required to implement an AEA.

Conclusion

IT organizations should strive for a modern computing architecture. When there is a need for global operations, the team designs the architectural to allow a continuous or 7x24 operation. Today's technical architecture is a combination of hardware, operating systems and network software. Collectively a BPM/BR strategy works as a series of loosely connected services. IT teams use the BPM/BR strategy to create applications that leverage these services.

There are many design choices to consider in building, upgrading or modernizing the enterprise architecture. Powerful and complex technologies complicate the decisions. The team in the technical architecture activity selects the physical components for a loosely connected EAI environment. Your team should consider parallel or grid architectures for scalability and consolidation of outdated hardware, and single application servers. Another choice is the new, low cost, high performance systems. These systems offer improved operations and simplified backup and recovery.

Separate teams manage processes for many legacy systems. Until organizations modernize, the old ways of supporting these systems must be preserved. The BPM/BR strategy can improve the efficiency of the technical architecture. Modernizing the technical infrastructure with BPM can unify these teams and cut manual steps (Chapter 6). Business process management software can replace legacy processes with a centralized control and messaging tracking for traceability, encryption and security.

Today's software includes many capabilities that lower development and production costs. Software for user applications and business intelligence includes database servers, managed query environment, web servers and portals. Increasingly high quality open source solutions are available for these.

A series of EAI, work flow, and document management applications support the core processes of the enterprise. There are many more capabilities in commercial application servers, such as BEA or WebSphere. Underneath this are databases, development frameworks, programming languages, and repositories. These tools are exquisite in their extensive and overlapping powers; however, they require massive amounts of programming in Java or C to work.

Business process and business rules software support business to business collaborations with very little programming. For instance, if a partner interacts with a contracting process in the enterprise, the transaction interacts with the business rules, run by a business rules engine and a business process, run by the process engine. The challenge in combining these capabilities is to select the solution set that best meets your design and support needs and is reasonably consistent.

You should consider the emerging role of wireless mobile devices. As the global wireless networks improve, there are new opportunities for rapid data collection capabilities and software with tactical capacities. These remote devices need to use mobile autonomous processes and agents.

In conclusion, the strategic benefits of composite application include:

- Application logic, functions, and features can be inserted, extracted, updated, and rearranged within a flexible, coordinated environment.
- The functionality of existing applications within the enterprise infrastructure can be extended, regardless of whether they are packaged applications, such as SAP, Oracle, or PeopleSoft, or are existing legacy applications and systems.
- Widely adopted industry standards can be leveraged to create a technology- and vendor-agnostic platform.
- Business processes in a network of partners or internal systems can be connected.
- Companies can adapt easily to changing customer needs and business climates rather than relying on manual integration or brittle point-to-point connections.

Businesses can configure and assemble Web Services to achieve tangible business value in months rather than years.

Clearly, today's IT infrastructure is an environment in flux. Over time, management's goal should be to improve the productivity and cut the cost and complexity of operating information technology. More robust technologies must be added to the ecosystem to remove older or unsupported hardware and software, consolidate redundancy, create easier relations with trading partners and take advantage of more profitable business practices. These technologies might include new COTS, operational systems got from mergers and takeovers. A simple vision is that IT managers should remove all the point-to-point integrations and replace them with technologies that don't require programming. The long-term vision is that all external components of the composite application will have synchronized, seamless access to the enterprise.

Data warehouses and the ETL that supports these should be automatically coordinated with changes to new business processes and rules. Managers should be able to implant special offerings or contract terms and respond to competitive offerings in an unconstrained way.

BPM/BR is a method for achieving this.

CHAPTER EIGHT

Transition

Once the project teams complete the activities of business process modeling, business rules, Business Intelligence and IT convergence, they move the products into production. Also, IT teams need a fast and efficient change-over process when transitioning from a legacy business process or application. To cut risks, you should carefully plan the transition.

The following information is based on extensive experience with BPM/BR transitions. This chapter describes how to plan for a BPM/BR transition or migration. It will help your team in the change-over process, save you on unnecessary expenses, and highlight the stages needed for a smooth and safe process.

Four phases complete the transition process:

- Transition plan: Your IT team should develop a thoughtful plan for moving the products of the BPM/BR into production,
- Migration of legacy processes: Legacy processes might affect the transition process,
- Testing and validation: An independent validation and verification team tests new systems or updates,
- BPM/BR Activation: After testing, the system migrates to the production environment.

This plan assumes that you have installed the software components of the BPM/BR. They should be in the organization's development, test and production environments.

Setting up a BPM/BR environment is not a small chore. Administrators need to be familiar with the installation procedures and considerations of:

- BPM Software, SeeBeyond, Intalio and others,

- BPM/BR Software, PEGA, Corticon, and others,
- BI Software, BusinessObjects, Cognos and others

They should learn the similarities and differences between the original environments. As part of the installation process, the managers create all new administrative jobs and tasks. The jobs need proper scheduling to maintain operation of the BPM/BR architecture.

Transition Activities

In the transition, the team prepares a system for the new or updated components. Ideally, in mature systems, this should be a simple matter of redeploying business processes and business rules. The systems that must be migrated should include development, testing and production.

Changes in business rules might require a migration of schema. If these changes mandate the addition or removal of data elements or constraints, then the database will need to change. Reports and stored procedures will need to adapt to changes in column names and constraints. For instance, process changes might phase out older batch processes. This calls for cutover to a more streamlined message—one with more succinct data elements. This can be a time-consuming and risky activity where larger databases are involved. The administration team needs to coordinate this activity with business operations.

During the migration the old system will clear outstanding processes. This might take several days or it might occur on a fiscal time boundary such as end of month.

As your application becomes more service-oriented, migration will become a simple task. Business rules tools can position predicate (If then else) changes for 'real-time', in-line updates. For instance if there is a threshold value that triggers a condition for a process, and the value is in a predicate, then you republish the rule in real time.

If there are changes to the application, database or messaging structure, then you should write a migration plan. The migration plan should include the timing of database changes and a tactical plan for letting the production system cut over to the new environment.

Transition Planning

As a first step for a success, you should plan the transition process. In earlier activities the team documented old process information and potential logic conflicts. You also need to understand your organization's technical architecture.

The team transitions affected operational data stores or data warehouses. After that, the organization's IT team starts the conversion process.

A successful migration needs a competent team to administer, start and use the new process. You should choose a team leader for the migration team. This team should include the current support staff, operators, production analysts, database administrators, product administrators, programming personnel, and security administrators.

In the BPM/BR or IT convergence activity, the process team documented the workflow of the old process steps. The BPM software manages the new process. But, steps of the old process need to be considered in the migration plan.

The migration team should develop a detailed maintenance schedule for the transition. The plan should identify the risks involved, so it can assure system availability.

A process workflow depicts completion of the critical aspects of application management. This workflow identifies where the old process can be ended and the new started. The migration plan should incorporate\ the Service Level Agreement (SLA) constraints.

Team Profile

The transition team should be familiar with the legacy systems features and operation. This includes the old system's methods of managing the environment, the site's rules, procedures, naming conventions and clerical chores.

Previous Process Management Assessment

For a safe transition to the new applications your team should:

- Identify how scheduling processes is performed in the current system and the operating system.
- Identify the people responsible for the old process.
- Create a list of all users, errors, system logs and software interfaces that are replaced.
- Provide lists of processes that run on a daily, weekly or monthly basis.

- Document process definitions that are in use and obsolete job definitions.
- Identify unsatisfactory scheduling definitions and executions.

Scheduling Environment

The team should analyze the impact on the organization's major operational systems. They consider the size, complexity and value to the business. The team should be aware of bottlenecks or constraints in the old processes. They should identify all manual schedules or coordination taken to maintain the system.

To do this they should document:

- The way administrators manage systems, personnel and schedules.
- Peak activity times and the number of processes that run during these times.
- The number of processes that use CRON, DBMS_JOB and other features and the types of automation used.
- Processes that are scheduled using dataset triggers, file arrival, and others.

Organizations have developed systems without standard commands and messaging structures. Your administrative staff may not have documented the process dependencies. As you remove applications or move them into the BPM/BR environment, you will discover these hidden facts. The process of formally defining the communications and sequential requirements is not only a transition task—it is a knowledge management task.

Develop details for each process. The outcome is to create a procedural outline for the operational system. You need this to validate process outcomes, resolve incidents or provide system administration warning. The result is a process review, built for proactive maintenance activities.

Transition Plan Results

The results of transition planning are:

- A list of the conversion team, including a team leader
- Software/hardware configuration map

- Identification of functionality gaps between BPM/BR and the methods being replaced
- Completed security matrix
- Outline of implementation strategy

Migration of Legacy Processes

If the legacy processes are part of the project, then these need to be part of the transition to a new system. In migration, the old schedule information should be moved into business process control. You find old scheduling and process coordination information in legacy practices. These include DBMS_JOBS, crontab, programs and scripts. The new business process is responsible for this coordination. The scheduling definitions are input into BPM/BR scheduling definitions through the BPM monitor.

Your administrators need to tune and adjust the BPM suite using enterprise management tools. When migrating many legacy practices, I recommend that one or two applications be chosen as pilots. By carrying out a pilot, the employees involved in the conversion have the opportunity to become familiar with BPM on a smaller scale.

In the pilot, BPM should monitor a few scheduled or event driven processes. The pilot should be business processes typical of the organization. It should also simulate typical scheduling complexities, job flow structure and interactions with other applications. A successful pilot implementation is the foundation for replacing the rest of the site's legacy processes.

BPM/BR supports either phased or full conversions, providing the ability to convert one process at a time or the entire enterprise center at once.

Migration of Legacy Processes Results

The results of migration of legacy processes are:

- Process schedule tables.
- Calendars of procedures and events.
- Old system documentation.

Testing and Validation

An independent testing team should validate the project's deliverables. They should perform regression testing on a separate test environment. Independent teams provide an unbiased view of the quality of the development efforts. This approach improves the confidence in the system. Before starting application validation, the technical team and the business system users should develop and agree testing procedures and documentation. Some Business Process Management tools and business rules repositories can develop queries and use-case steps that generate test scenarios.

Testing is simplified when the applications architecture is built with loose coupling. There are fewer dependencies among the parts of the applications. Service oriented architecture improves stability because each component can be proven to function according to the requirements. In this way, capability is verified in a cumulative way.

Application validations can build confidence in the immediate application while cutting the downstream testing efforts.

Regression testing is a type of testing that attempts to exercise all features of an application. The testing team can develop scripts with regression testing tools such as Rational Robot™.

The business rules repository holds metadata that describe how a system interacts with users and processes. The analysts develop test use cases with queries against the business rules repository. They also collect validation data sets.

After the team assembles data and scripts, the system should be validated through independent testing and validation. The independent team is responsible for the setup and testing areas harmonization. As they conduct the testing, they create deficiency reports and work with the organization to identify corrective measures.

If the project involves new business processes, interfaces and rules then the team should do unit, integration, and acceptance testing. Simple changes to business processes or business rules might not need rigorous testing.

Disciplined testing is critical for successful deployment of any complicated system. The separate roles of business process and business rules simplifies some of the complexities of testing. How organizations test their system depends on the project's goals. Yet there are common methods of testing. In general, developers test products of their activities during the phases of the BPM/BR. Testing the entire system requires coordination.

Table 8.1 describes the types of testing that must be performed in a business process, business rules and Business Intelligence environment:

Type	Description
Process unit testing	Testing of the flows of the business process. Test messaging control.
Business rules unit testing	Test business rules against business cases.
Business Intelligence unit testing	Test metrics against the computed benchmarks in the test data set.
Business Process and business rules integration testing	Load business processes with data from business cases that exercise rules with expected outcomes.
Business process and interface integration testing	Verify target system receives expected business process inputs and translations are correct
Business Intelligence and ETL process testing	Verify that test transactions feed data warehouse schema properly
Acceptance testing	Verify application meets business requirements

Acceptance testing is done by or in conjunction with people for whom the system is being created. Often these are the persons who use the system when it is put in production.

The team conducts unit and integration tests in the phases of the BPM/BR. Acceptance testing is done as a final check before putting the system into production.

Test Plan

The requirements of the system direct the system testing. A test plan is created in the transition planning phase. This test plan specifies how the system is tested and what requirements the system must meet before it is put into production.

The functional and technical specifications outline the exact procedure used to conduct the tests, both at a component level and at an integrated system level. These specifications include:

- Type of data to use
- Expected output
- Who is responsible for the test

Test Data Sets

A complete test plan specifies the test data sets. At the unit and the integration levels, your team should use data that follow scenarios that reflect the business process. Where possible, test data sets should come from legacy systems. The scenarios should exercise as many process paths as possible. In addition to real-life data, create data designed to test the system's error handling. You might manually construct or generate this data.

Performance testing needs large volumes of data. The volume of data should match the conditions of business operations.

Test Plan Results

The test plan includes specifications for:

- Exceptions handling
- Transaction performance
- Flow of information
- Transformation of data
- Test data sets, business scenarios and volume testing

Unit Testing

In unit testing, developers verify their work before integration testing. Each part of the system must be unit-tested before the component becomes part of the new application or process. It is useful to develop a unit testing procedure as a part of the technical specifications. In the absence of test procedures, the developer should verify their part performs according to the specifications.

Integration Testing

Integration testing verifies that new components work together and in the organization's environment. If the system is complex, you should divide the testing into steps. The steps should test a part of the system. For instance you might verify that transactions move from a file to an interface. A partial test would be to verify the data can be sent from the file to the interface.

Performance Testing

Often, performance testing follows integration testing. Integration testing validates a system's expected operation. Performance testing verifies the adequacy of the system's speed. The testers should test system performance after the system is correctly working.

Another aim of performance testing is to find the bottlenecks in the system. A composite of many factors affect performance. Because of unknown obstructions, tuning a slow process or rule might not improve system performance. Uncovering these bottlenecks shows developers where to improve processing speeds.

In the test plan, the organization should estimate expected and peak volumes. This volume will define the needed performance level.

Stress Testing

The testing team conducts stress testing to decide if the system can handle the expected load. With stress testing, the testers overload the system with data to the point of failure. Stress tests process operationally significant transaction volumes, and multiple concurrent connections. This is another effective way to uncover network bottlenecks.

Acceptance Testing

Before moving the system into production, users should validate the system as complying with requirements and specifications. You might do acceptance testing for a part of the system or for an entire system. A typical acceptance strategy specifies the capabilities a system needs in order to go into production. You should also specify who must "sign off" on the new process.

Parallel Testing

It is important to assure integrity of the organization's production process flow. The testing team tests each process before production activation. This might be part of a phased conversion process rather than converting all processes at once.

Following the conversion process, new business processes should be activated in parallel to the old process methods. In this phase, BPM software simulates the production application's operations.

Testing should schedule processes to run in the test environment rather than production. The production managers can validate that business process software will correctly coordinate or schedule the production processes. This should match production system operation. Final processes validation occurs through examination of records and logs.

Testing Results

The results of testing are:

- Activation of processes in test environment mode to simulate processes in production environment in parallel with the old environment
- Adjustment and validation of converted elements
- Review of organization's support staff skills
- Organization's staff is familiar with BPM/BR

Production

If the project is a new business process then the branching and networking of each activity should be balanced with service level requirements. If you can isolate an activity as a unit, then you can evaluate compliance with SLA constraints. For instance, an activity runs in parallel after a financial application has closed the accounts on a billing period. Other processes might need the updated data to finish.

After completing all previous phases, the organizations business should run with new business process. At this stage, the organizations IT systems should switch from the old process to the new application.

Production Results

The results of production are

- Activation of converted elements in 'production' mode
- On-site support and fine-tuning during the transition phase
- Completion and delivery of operation guide

Summary

Once a process or business rule is in production, there are more considerations. A Business Process Management approach creates loosely coupled applications, and this can change the systems architecture.

In the chapter on IT convergence, I described a strategy for unified scheduling and controlling processes. Unified process control is an important part of Business Process Management. Adopting BPM will need a migration of different needs across scattered systems. Many operational systems are a myriad of processes, data feed loads, and extracts that have become difficult to support. These all feed the IT ecosystem. Many organizations are dependent on a team of technical personnel to monitor and control this complicated environment. An aim of BPM, in the IT convergence phase, is to improve this. The BPM team can add new capabilities and improve service conditions for your users. In this environment, there is a driving need for an integration of the processes that is accessible by nontechnical managers and administrators.

With the system in production, administrators should monitor system activity, check for errors, and change configurations. Monitoring system activity is critical for the long-term success of the system. Routine checks measure long-term performance benchmarks. Such benchmarks help in identifying undesirable changes. If you cannot identify a healthy system's vital signs, you will not know when your system needs attention.

The test environment is the only mature way to verify and refine the system configuration that was set up earlier in the deployment process. Focusing on the transition plan ensures the smoothest possible deployment. By thoroughly unit testing and system testing in the test environment, you will avoid costly errors and the end users will be satisfied with the results.

CONCLUSIONS

Conclusion

Six months have passed and Sumter has entered the production phase of new processes for maintenance management, customer relations and business intelligence for inventory management. Equipment managers have shifted from working with reams of printouts and clipboards to focusing on the needs of their customers. The simplicity of the system has rooted out many hidden problems. The IT process team has added all retail stores. Because SAP PM has accurate odometer data, Sumter managers see a clearer snapshot of the age and condition of the rental fleet.

With the new customer relationship process, Sumter negotiated discounts with over 50 of the largest construction firms in their service area. Armed with reports and the new business intelligence tools, managers can evaluate the benefit of each of these contracts—do these customers lease more equipment for longer periods of time. The new process writes a record when a customer cannot reserve the equipment they need. Retail managers are looking at this data. They have found that verbal contact with the customer is best after they tried to reserve equipment three times. Because of this feature, local stores have improved their sales.

The business intelligence system is yielding many tactical benefits. In one example, a regional manager found a city with several large residential construction projects. It came from an analysis of high lease use rates of the bulldozers normally used in residential construction. Sumter managers were able to move underutilized equipment to the affected stores. This is an example of how business intelligence and business area monitoring produce timely information that can be used for tactical business advantages.

The BPM/BR has positioned Sumter's critical rules and processes for change. For instance managers can add rules that direct store personnel to call customers after their third try to reserve an equipment type. This change can happen without programming. Sumter has discovered through BI and insight gained from the recent changes that average time from order to delivery is 2 weeks. Since average transport time is only 2 days, managers aim to improve the paperwork intensive process of transporting large orders. Sumter management will target order fulfillment for the next round of BPM/BR improvements. Management believes that a new order process will cut fulfillment to 1 week resulting in a revenue increase of $5 million for each year.

Six months into Sumter's First BPM/BR project, the critical metric for the return on investment, actual lease rates (ALR), is improving. Each percentage of improvement in the ALR improves profitability by %2-3. The ROI target was to improve the ALR by %1.

The business of equipment leasing has many complex interactions. Profit margins are connected to a combination of business operations, economic demand and Sumter's ability to tune equipment inventory. There are many equipment types; some targeted for narrow construction needs. Also, construction varies seasonally. Combining business process improvements, business rules and business intelligence yields powerful investigation tools for these dynamic interactions. Also, improvements can be quantified.

Finally, the CIO takes a two-week vacation.

Discussion

I have spoken much about Business Process Management and Business Rules Approach (BPM/BR). Part of my aim with this book was to show you how you use these techniques to create and maintain your applications. The techniques create solutions with little traditional programming. Using BPM/BR is simple: Business rules and business processes meets your critical needs. BPM/BR also manages and maintains the operational system after it is in production. This approach changes the activities of the development team from the traditional engineering process to the business needs of the application it is supporting.

Even organization have not discovered them, each has business rules and business processes that are unique. I call these the 'cultural' practices. BPM/BR's purpose is to create a composite application for the cultural practices. For instance, a retailer, bank or telecommunication's company might use SAP as its ERP; however, it develops its own web storefront for branding and other competitive reasons. The web application is a part of the business process and must interact with the business rules. BPM/BR does this for you.

In the past a business process was tightly bound to the system that performed the reports and accounting. To change the system, developers must change all computer programs that move data from one system to another.

The BPM/BR easily adapts to new or changing rules and processes because the components of the system not tightly bound. Web services create the loose binding. With web services, process, rules or system interfaces are published as a specification. Organizations that do this are moving to Business process language (BPEL). Processes orchestrate web services with BPEL.

Business analysts who are able to produce finished business solutions create the solution with the BPM/BR. These 'super users' use the BPM/BR design environment to create prototypes to solve a problem. The traditional role of the development team is to carry out requirements, separate from the business experts. This approach brings the business personnel into the development process and the results are efficient. This is what the IT industry call self-service because it provides rapid acknowledgments when it immediately shows the results of adjustments to a business rule.

Like most methods, a team uses the BPM/BR to develop applications in a repetitive, interlocking process. The BPM/BR process is comprehensive because it builds all the parts of today's IT environment in the cycle. It develops by refining business processes, then business rules, then integrations and Business Intelligence components. What most distinguishes a BPM/BR approach from other cyclical methods is that commercial software packages play a vital role in developing the integration architecture. These packages include BPM suite, business rules engines, managed query environments and ERP's.

The BPM/BR team delivers solid IT solutions with a round-trip industrial process. This process draws on the disciplines of methodology, quality, and domain know-how. Figure 9.1 presents the components of what I call composite application factory. Each of the triangles represents a virtual workstation. As they design changes to the composite system, knowledge workers sit at workstations and model business processes and business rules, and BI, then evaluate and publish the results. There is little coding because the designers specifications become the program. Work flows from workstation to workstation through a series of environments. In this environment, methodology, transition quality, and domain know-how allow the activities to be well coordinated and efficient-. Methodology, transition and domain environments allow the work to be efficient, correct, productive. The environments of methodology, transition, and domain expertise provide the delivery mechanisms for the work flows.

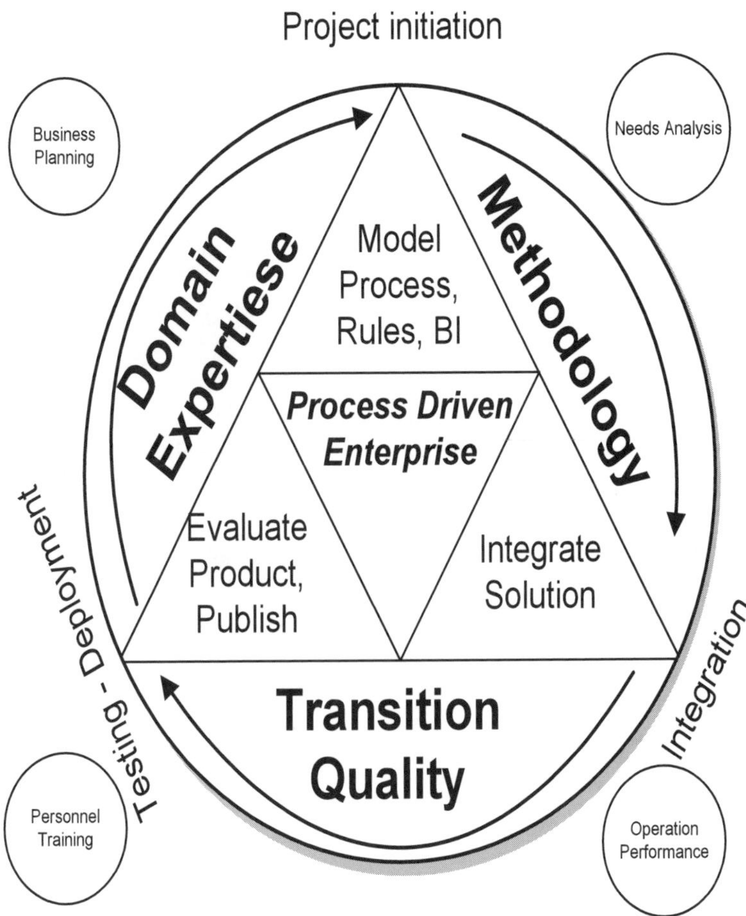

Figure 9.1 The BPM/BR is a simplified method of selecting the right software integrating the components of an EAI environment. Commercial software (COTS) plays a vital role in the architecture.

An important part of the entire deployment project is change management. If changes are needed, they must be processed through the same cycle of planning, development, testing, transition to production, and maintenance as the rest of the deployment.

The Performance Gap Between Technology and IT Management

I see the gap among business objectives and the old methods of information technology as similar to recent technological changes in the television industry. In the past five years, the changes in the cable and satellite television industry have been dramatic. There is video on demand, interactive services, even integration with web technology. Yet, look at how long it is has taken the US industry and government to create digital television standards for broadcast signals. The technological realities—decades old standards, broadcast frequencies, analog infrastructures—have been in competition with the new ways of bringing television to the public.

As with many new technologies High Definition Television (HDTV), is the subject of a bureaucratic struggle among competing interests. Much of the struggle has been over the gargantuan piece of radio frequency, or bandwidth, occupied by the old standard. Television is broadcast on the airways across a 70-year old radio spectrum. This bandwidth, which might hold more than 100 channels for each analog channel, has the potential to host multitudes of channels for public and commercial communication. But, cable and satellite television carriers would prefer to avoid the competition. This unrealized capacity could create a massive, new communication infrastructure for the public's use. The self-interests of licensed broadcasters, cable television operators and others have clashed with the government objectives in creating fair use for the radio spectrum.

On a project that managed the communication's spectrum for DoD I learned that the television's spectrum occupies an enormous space in our airways. It will be years if not decades until it becomes available for modern use. (See http://www.ntia.doc.gov/osmhome/allochrt.html)

The airway bandwidth occupied by the old TV standards is a metaphor for a business IT system. It has existed for many years and it performs a valuable role; however the delivery of the capabilities and information is wasteful. It is too expensive and time-consuming. The competing interests and objectives of software companies, business managers and IT delivery teams have created a business risk of adopting new IT technology. The risk is that proposed or mandated changes in a corporate method climate might unleash a wasteful struggle for the funding, personnel, power and authority. For instance, supporters of aged software systems, tools and methods (programming in the small) might prefer to avoid the competition. Exposing interfaces and processes to the Enterprise as web services (programming in the large) removes the mystery of how a system works and that encourages a competitive environment. Because organizations have poorly integrated and fragile software, much of this conflict is affixed to staying in the past. This results in a low return on investment (ROI). Also, there is a shortage of properly trained professionals to improve the IT ecosystem. Because operational managers are already busy running the business, they are reluctant to take on the added efforts needed to adopt commercial software that do BPM and The Business Rules Approach. Also, the legacy system might be abandoned or parts of it must be replaced by smaller applications and integrations to the new software. Adding a competitive practice, one that can improve the productivity of the business, is similarly difficult.

The potential of improved management practices including Business Process Management, business rule, and Business Intelligence software, modern machinery for competing in the economy, is arguably similar to the communication bandwidth occupied by television broadcasters. Both of these potentials are underutilized. Both of these will reap vast rewards for society, and second, economic efficiencies dictate their use. Just as government and private broadcasters interest must finally agree on the television bandwidth, so the corporation must strive to keep its IT infrastructure integrated, efficient and competitive. IT must align enterprise IT ecosystems with modern practices in the face of a tangled world of operational, legacy and ERP systems. So I refer to the new technology stacks, commercial software, Business Intelligence tools, integration tools and hardware as *competitive bandwidth*—an environment that is perfectly formed.

The Mandate of Business Process Management and Business Rules

For all enterprises, including governments and non-profits, there is a basic principle that should be in their IT strategy—business software must efficiently use the competitive bandwidth available to them. To do this, whenever they can they should lower the cost of in-house systems by replacing them with commercial ERP software products.

For the rest of their operational applications, data warehousing and, integrations, they should look to the methods of Business Rules and Business Process Management. This means that your programming staff should stop programming 'in the small'. The rest of the IT needs of the enterprise should be built with methods that adapt to the changes that are cost effective and efficient through all business cycles.

Remember Mr. Carr's comment that the biggest risk to IT is overspending. If you are not using Business Process Management, then someone in your organization is creating programs in Java, C#, and others that do this. If you are not using business rules software, then someone in your organization is creating programs that do this—or worse yet they are scattering business rules across a slew of programs.

To expand their use of this competitive bandwidth, organizations should cutout outdated models of problem solving and create an architecture that is synchronized. By synchronized, I mean that the systems do what the business needs it to do, not what legacy systems developers had it do. Synchronization is carried out with a method that provides business managers with the information technology they need. In this book, I have suggested that you can deliver this by adapting a strategy that with a combination of Business Process Management and Business Rules Approach (BPM/BR). I have described how these new tools improve construction of the application, integrations, and Business Intelligence. The result is a powerful system that saves the organization's time and money by allowing it to operate the system with a smaller, more skilled staff and shorter development cycles.

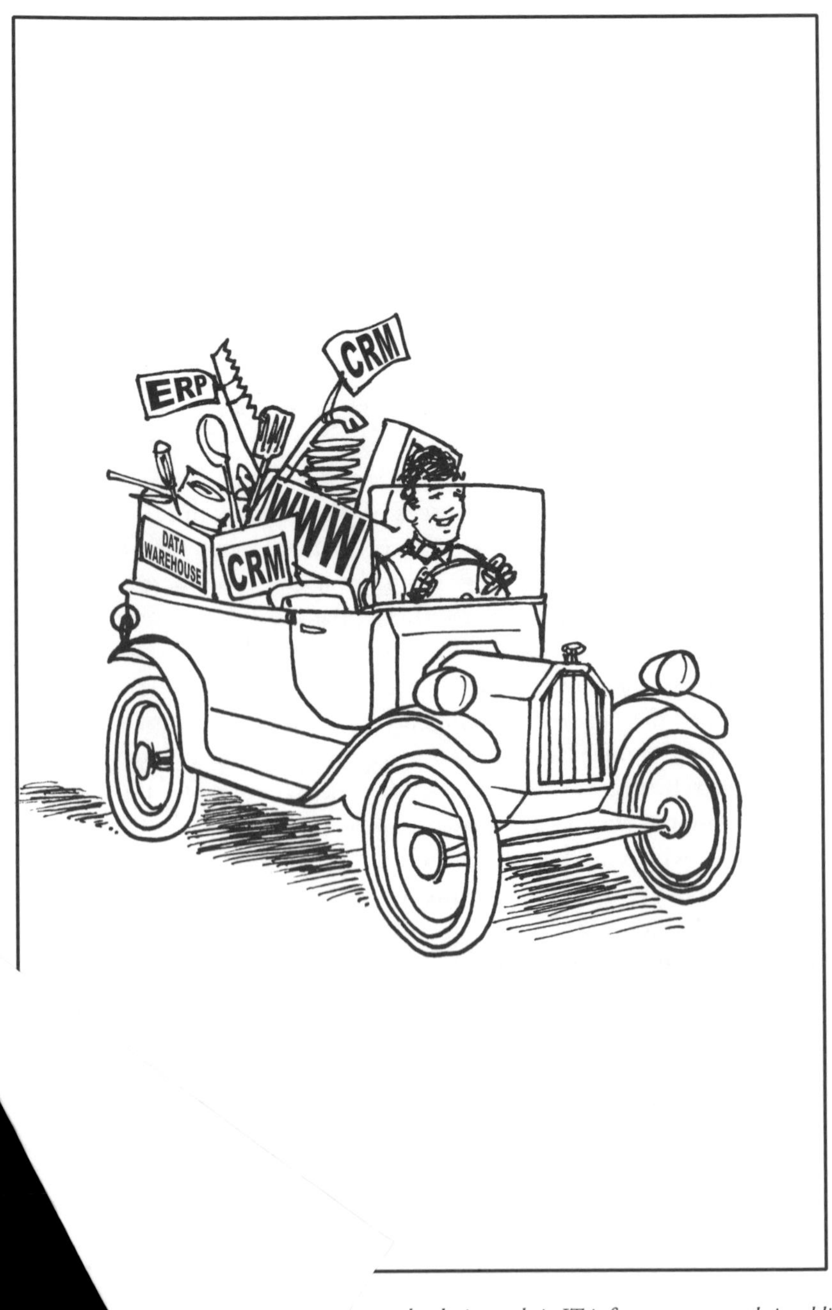

rent technologies to their IT infrastructure, yet their addi-
its that they wanted.

The BPM/BR modernizes the way today's business information architectures are built. It replaces outmoded ways of developing the IT environment. Organizations have hung competitive, technologies from their enterprise IT ecosystem with hardwired retrofit style methods. These retrofits resulted in a rigid technical architecture. The BPM/BR overcomes this past by addressing integration, data warehousing and applications in one step. It avoids retrofitting the environment by creating loosely coupled components whose connections can help new solutions, commercial software or analytical tools.

The new models suggested by BPM with business rules potentially have cut or ended the need to program many artifacts. It includes:

- Business process management (BPM): A management technology that models the core processes of the enterprise and isolates them from the systems that are responsible for them
- Business Rules Approach: A technique of describing, modeling and forming engines that interpret the constraints, policies and basic data needs of the enterprise
- Exposure of the components as web services to the right organizations in and outside the organization. This enables the composite application, a series of independent systems and capabilities that appear unified to the users and customers.

Commercial off-the-shelf (COTS) software has modernized many systems, and these also must be integrated.

SUMMARY

When a designer solves a problem domain he begins by creating an abstract model. For a solution to be worthy, its model must be able to adapt to reasonable changes to the requirements without doing great violence to the core of the assumptions. In computer science, the abstraction provides an accommodation to a programming problem, expressed in the data structures and code. The levels and degree of abstraction allow the solution to contribute to all the requirements that surround the problem domain. Business process modeling and business rules is an abstraction of business. Yet so is computer code. There is a fundamental difference.

The act of listening to a musical composition is an expression of the monoidal nature of consciousness. The composer inscribes, with pen and paper, the notes of the music; musicians perform the music at a recording studio, and its sound becomes output for the listener to enjoy. Each artifact—the paper manuscript, the performance and the listening experience—is a form of the same item. It is not inconceivable that the listener could come up with a technique for recreating the manuscript by hearing the recorded media; similarly, an ensemble, or performer, could reproduce a performance from such an auditory experience. Paper notations of musical ideas have a 'convertible basis' from the data shared across representations.

Business information, including processes, rules and metrics, is a convertible basis of capabilities in the enterprise. BPEL is a modeling form that reflects a business process. It is a document that reflects a process diagram that depicts a physical process. Methods, like Business Process Management, have their roots in business practices. It is easy to imagine how a business process moves from the business process modeling diagram to the truck delivering inventory, or a factory producing products. It is not so easy imagining a huge pile of Java or C# making the same leap.

The objective of an abstract, monoidal design is to allow core business processes to be transformed seamlessly into applications, interfaces and business facts. These transformations are created through abstracting business process, rules and intelligence.

In this book, I have described the important activities of this composite method (BPM/BR) and the important roles of the team members that approach these problems. I have contrasted the BPM/BR with the outdated methodologies by showing how it incorporates new standard practices into developing and maintaining the IT ecosystem. The contrast is the in the abstractions afforded by these methods.

GLOSSARY

Activities: An activity is a business process component that performs a specific function. In a business process diagram, activities include the programs that process data, services from applications and web services. Flow control is also a type of activity.

Activity Instances: An invoked instance of an activity in a business process, as invoked by the business process suite.

Adapter: An adapter is software that works with Business Process Management suites. Adapters provide prepackaged services for ERPs and transaction standards. Adapters simplify integration.

Alignment/Performance Gap: A discrepancy between a business strategy or model and the services that the systems provide. A BPM/BR project corrects this discrepancy.

Automated BPEL: The part of BPEL that describes software services and utilities.

Binding Service: In WSDL, the term binding service refers to the process associating protocol or data format information with an abstract entity like a message, operation, or portType.

BPM Suite: Software that comprehensively designs and manages business processes and monitors their execution.

Business Activity Monitoring: The combination of Business Process Management and Business Intelligence. Business activity monitoring implies real time data.

Business Case: The Business Case addresses, at a high level, the business need that the project seeks to resolve. It includes the reasons for the project, the expected business benefits, the options considered (with reasons for rejecting or carrying forward each option), and the expected costs of the project.

Business Intelligence: an umbrella term for a set of concepts and methods to improve business decision making by using a fact based system.

Business Intelligence supports business strategy by creating a tool for measuring and tuning the outcome.

Business Model: the mechanism by which a business intends to generate revenue and profits. For government and non-profits it is the mechanism by which the organization intends to carry out its mission.

Business Process: A sequence of activities that carries out a goal and is complete in some way. It is a full orchestration of activities that has an important aim or purpose.

Business Process Management (BPM): The identification, understanding and management of business processes that link with people and systems in and across organizations

Business Process Extended Language (BPEL): the Business Process Execution Language (BPEL) is a programming language, serialized in XML, that is intended to enable the high level state transition logic of a process.

BPML Business process modeling language: A standard created by the Business Process Management organization for graphically describing BPEL. BPML is done in graphical user interfaces.

Business Rule: The mediator of computer systems or people, such as managers, employees and salespeople, that decides with information. Example: a policy, a constraint or regulatory requirement

Business Rule Approach (BR): A design technique for formalizing an enterprises critical business rules in a language the manager and technologist understand.

Business Rule Repository (BRR): Software and data structures that retain and configure business rules. Metadata in the BRR provides instructions to an instance of a business rule, run by the rules engine.

Business Strategy: A plan or campaign that a business or organization uses to carry out their business model.

Candidate Project: In business architecture, this is a project that might align IT systems with a performance gap or other needs.

Collection: In business rules, this is an array or record set.

Computation: In business rules, formulas, selections of data such as the maximum or minimum value, or statistical trends. In this text, transformations are considered computations.

Cubes: In Business Intelligence, or data warehousing, a cube is the mapping between the data that stores the facts and dimensions and the information that describes prompts and column headings (metadata). The cube is also a user-friendly connection between a manager's point and click and the technical query.

Data Structures: In business rules, a data structure is a database table or data source that the rule uses to create records in an operational data store.

Data Warehouse: A set of database tables that hold the dimensions and facts, the MQE, and the processes that populate and manage the data.

Decision Table: In business rules, a decision table is a data-driven collection of predicates (if ... then ... else), designed to be easily manipulated by business users.

Dimensions: In Business Intelligence, a holder of descriptive detail, including types, categories, or a named entities (customers, orders, and others) from the business ideas.

Enterprise: A business, government, or non profit organization that has a mission.

ETL processes: A type of business process that performs extraction loading and transformation of data into a data warehouse.

Exception: In BPEL, an exception is an unexpected system, process or data failure.

Exceptions Management: In Business Process Management, a procedure for notification, elevation and communication of process exceptions.

Executive Dashboard: In Business Intelligence, a graphical depiction of executive decision metrics.

External System: In Business Process Management, a system that exists outside the enterprises.

Fact: In Business Intelligence, a numeric attribute that is associated with a dimension. Facts are also called measures. Facts are usually numerical inputs into metrics.

Flow Control: In BPEL, a flow control is an activity that directs other activities in the processes. Examples of flow control include switch statements and while loops.

Input Message: In business rules WSDL, the data that the business rule needs to evaluate a rule.

Internal System: In process management, a system in the enterprise ecosystem.

Invoked Apps: In process management, an application that a process needs services from.

Managed Query Environment: Commercial software that provides tools for building and managing cubes, executive dashboards and reports.

Manual: In BPML a manual process is a process that takes personnel to finish.

Metrics: A system of parameters or ways of quantitative assessment of a business model or process that is to be measured, along with the processes to carry out such measurement. Metrics define what is to be measured. Metrics are usually specialized by the business model or strategy. Metrics assess the present state of business and prescribe course of action.

Modified Terms: In business rules, specialized types or categories.

MQE Web Service: A web services interface to the MQE.

Multidimensional Schema: A table layout that is developed from multidimensional analysis is a design that groups data into two basic categories: dimensions and facts. Multidimensional analysis supports the ability to execute a multidimensional query that supports the summarized data across one or more nested, logical groups.

Operation: In WSDL, an operation is the function that you invoke when running the web service. A WSDL may have many operations.

Operational Data Store: A database designed to integrate data from many sources to simplify operations, analysis and reporting.

Output Message: In WSDL the output of a web services operation.

Partner: The part of BPEL that describes the programs and external services that are used by business processes.

Policies, Constraints (Offerings, Negotiations): The aggregate of the enterprise governance of a business model. Many explicit business rules enforce these.

Port type: In web services defines the exposed operations (similar to a function call in programming languages). Usually there is an input, an output and a default port type

Predicate Constraints: A predicate guard.

Predicates: In business rules, a statement of a business rules in an if ... then ... else form. Business rules predicates resolve to true or false.

Process and Systems Monitoring: Systems administration in a business process environment.

Process Instances: An instance of a running process that is developed from a process definition.

Process Utility: In the Business Process Management suite, activities use localized services to carry out basic functions such as

Rules Engine: In business rules software, the rules engine is the mechanism through which the business rules are run. Rules engine use the metadata, or rules schema, to develop the execution steps.

Rules Instances: An invocation of a business rule, as run by the rules engine.

Rules Schema: The metadata that retains business rules.

Rules Service: The web services interface to the business rule. The

Rules WSDL: An XML format for describing web services. Rules WSDL is the WSDL for a business rule.

Selected Project: A project deemed worthy of completion due to a solid business case.

Service Oriented Architecture (SOA): A concept that defines services used to support the requirements of software users. The architecture publishes resources to other participants in the network as independent services that the participants access in a standardized way. Most SOA definitions include web services.

Work Items: In Business Process Management, work items are activities that are assigned to users in a work flow system.

INDEX